Enjoy!
Bonnie A
4-9-11

COOKING WITH BONNIE:

Farm to France

BONNIE AESCHLIMAN

BONNIE AESCHLIMAN, CCP

Visit our website at www.farmtofrance.com
to receive notice of author events or to order
additional copies of this book.

For information about Bonnie's cooking school:

COOKING AT BONNIE'S PLACE
9747 EAST 21st STREET, SUITE 139
WICHITA, KANSAS 67206
3 1 6 . 4 2 5 . 5 2 2 4
www.cookingatbonnies.com

Text Copyright © 2011 Culinary Concepts
Photo Copyrights listed on page 223

First Edition: 2011

ISBN 10: 0-9634665-1-8
ISBN 13: 978-0-9634665-1-8

Printed in the United States of America

Book Design by SaraBeth Fillingane
ARTFULLY DONE BOOKS
Managing Editor: RoxAnn Banks Dicker

Food photography onsite by Gary Krohe
and RoxAnn Banks Dicker.
Additional photos by artists of
istockphoto.com and thinkstock.com
(credits listed on page 223) and historical
photos by Bonnie Aeschliman.
Back cover photo: Jeff Tuttle
Book flap photo: *The Wichita Eagle*

This cookbook contains recipes taught in cooking classes.
While most are original, some may be adaptations or inspired
by others. Every effort has been made to acknowledge all sources.
However, should any not be properly attributed, the publisher
will make appropriate corrections in future editions of the book.

DEDICATION

Lovingly dedicated to my children,
Eddie Aeschliman and Christy Aeschliman Lewis,
who have loved me, encouraged me,
and always made me proud of them.

TABLE *of* CONTENTS

MENUS

Spring & Summer

Fall & Winter

TABLE of CONTENTS
❋ RECIPES ❋

BEVERAGES

Melon Slush . 48
Ruby Slipper Sippers . 182

SOUPS & STEWS

Chef Claudio's Barley and Black-Eyed
  Pea Soup . 18
Cream of Carrot Soup . 27
Cream of Watercress Soup . 26
Spicy Spanish Gazpacho . 70
French Onion Soup . 126
Bonnie's Quick and Easy Chili . 150
Sherried Mushroom, Ham and Wild
  Rice Soup . 132
Roasted Butternut Squash Soup with Thyme
  and Cider Cream . 154
Pasta Fagiola . 168

BREADS & MUFFINS

Mini Lemon Poppy Seed Muffins . 52
Pesto Garlic Bread . 77
Crusty Garlic Cheese Herb Bread . 143
Cornbread Wedges with Scallions and
  Bacon . 149
Rosemary Focaccia . 172
Heavenly Crescent Rolls . 181
Homemade Cinnamon Rolls . 188
Cranberry Streusel Muffins . 193

SIDES & VEGETABLES

Porcini Mushroom Risotto . 19
Oven Roasted Vegetables . 20
Creamed New Potatoes and Peas . 29
Steamed Asparagus & Tomato Herb Salsa . 30
Fresh Green Beans Almondine . 35
Orzo Parmesan with Basil, Scallions and
  Peppers . 36
Coconut Cilantro Rice . 44
Cuban Black Beans with Tomato Salsa . 44
Zucchini and Sun-dried Tomato Tart . 51
Mexican Rice Risotto . 58
Roasted Corn, Zucchini, Peppers and
  Tomatoes . 58
New Potatoes in Dill and Chive Sauce . 64
Sautéed Zucchini and Grape Tomatoes . 65
Roasted New Potatoes with Horseradish . 79
Sautéed Summer Squash with Olives and
  Parmesan . 85
Cheese Ravioli with Garden-Ripe Tomatoes
  and Spinach . 87
Black Bean and Corn Salsa . 92
Texas Slaw . 92
Tall Texas Tater Towers . 94
Avocado, Tomato and Corn Salad . 98
Cilantro Rice . 102
Roasted Potatoes with Herbs . 107
Creamy Garlic Spinach . 108
Garlic Mashed Potatoes . 116
Roasted Corn, Zucchini and Chiles in
  Lime Butter . 122
Vanilla Roasted Sweet Potato Wedges . 122
Potatoes Dauphinois . 128
Pike County Fried Apples . 133
Broccoli with Toasted Garlic Crumbs . 133
Wild Rice and Vegetable Pilaf . 155
Cranberry Apricot Chutney . 156
Wild Rice with Dried Cranberries and
  Almonds . 161
Cauliflower Broccoli Gratin with Walnuts . 162
Green Bean Carrot Bundles with Bacon . 177
Potatoes Soufflé Gratinée . 179
Cinnamon and Pecan Roasted Apples . 185
Golden Potato Gratin with Goat Cheese . 213
Sautéed Green Beans with Bacon, Shallots
  and Mushrooms . 213

ENTREES

Roasted Rosemary and Sage Tenderloin of
  Pork . 21
Orange Glazed Baked Ham . 28
Roasted Salmon Roulade with Spinach Feta
  Filling . 37
Sweet and Spicy Glazed Pork Tenderloin . 43
Tarragon Chicken Salad . 50
Chipotle Glazed Roasted Pork Tenderloin . 57
Roasted Salmon with Lemon Butter Sauce . 63
New Orleans Muffuletta . 71
Marinated Rosemary Flank Steak . 78
Chicken Asiago Spedini . 86
Smoked and Slow-Braised Oven Barbecued
  Beef Brisket . 93
Sausage Quesadillas with Black Bean
  Salsa . 99
Shredded Beef Enchiladas with Salsa
  Verde . 100
Bourbon and Brown Sugar Marinated Strip
  Steaks . 109
Beef Bourguignon . 115
Smokin' Chile Pork Tenderloin with
  Cranberry Jezebel Sauce . 121
Roast Chicken with Herb Butter,
  Carrots and Onions . 127
Marinated Thick Pork Chops with
  Pan Sauce . 135
Oven Roasted Italian Meatballs in Long-
  Simmered Ragu Sauce . 142
Bonnie's Quick and Easy Chili . 150
Maple Smoked Chicken . 156
Roasted Loin of Pork with Blackberry
  Reduction . 163
Northern Italian Chicken Cannelloni with
  Two Sauces . 170
Herb Roasted Beef Tenderloin with
  Mushroom Gorgonzola Sauce . 178
Classic Kentucky Hot Browns . 186
Chicken Florentine Phyllo Pie . 194
Individual Beef Wellingtons . 212

DESSERTS

Fresh Churned Strawberry Gelato with
  Chocolate Hazelnut Sauce . 22
Strawberries and Cream Cake . 31
Blackberry Rippled Baked Alaska . 38
Key Lime Tart in Coconut Crust . 45
Pistachio Gelato . 53
Pumpkin Caramel Flan . 59
Peach Melba Tart . 66
Key Lime Bars . 73
Rustic Blackberry Cobbler . 80
Chocolate Hazelnut Torte . 88
Lone Star Sheet Cake with Chocolate
  Pecan Frosting . 95
Frozen Texas Tumbleweeds . 103
Chocolate Molten Lava Cakes with Vanilla
  Custard Sauce and Raspberry Coulis . 110
Individual Apple Tarts . 117
Coco Lopez Soufflé . 123
Pot de Crème with White Chocolate
  Whipped Cream . 129
White Chocolate Banana Cream Pie in
  Almond Crust . 136
Vanilla Bean Panna Cotta with Honey
  Berry Sauce . 145
Hot Lemon Soufflé with Raspberry
  Sauce . 157
Vanilla Bean Panna Cotta with Honey Berry
  Sauce . 145
Hazelnut White Chocolate Cheesecake . 164
Turtle Bars . 151
Lemon Swirl Cheesecake . 173
White Chocolate Raspberry Tiramisu with
  Chocolate Leaves . 180
Blueberry Lemon Bundt Cake . 196
Ultimate Cranberry Bars . 206
Chocolate Babycakes . 207
Chocolate Glazed Irish Cream
  Cheesecake . 214

Farm to France

A CULINARY JOURNEY

IT'S A LONG STRETCH from learning to cook in a rustic, Missouri farm kitchen to teaching a class in a French culinary school. But that's my life — an incredible culinary journey — and one that I invite you along on in *Cooking with Bonnie: Farm to France*. Whether you are a novice or an experienced cook, this book will guide you with beautifully planned menus and detailed recipes that will delight your family and friends through each season of the year.

OVER THE YEARS I have been privileged to have hundreds of students come to my kitchen for cooking classes. In *Cooking with Bonnie: Farm to France* you will find favorite recipes from those classes. Together, we cooked our way through the seasons of the year, creating tantalizing recipes that could easily be reproduced in their own kitchens. It seemed only natural for me to teach menu-based classes so the students would learn how to make a meal from start to finish. The bonus was sharing a delicious meal at the conclusion of the cooking. As students returned to learn new techniques and cuisines, deep friendships evolved. Food, whether the preparation or the enjoyment of it, has a way of opening doors and making many memories.

THIS BOOK HAS EVOLVED along with my experiences — it is a cookbook based upon my rural roots but embraces many urban styles and cuisines that I have experienced and taught for many years. In *Cooking with Bonnie: Farm to France*, I kept the menu format so that you, too, will be able to assemble a complete meal, with easy-to-follow recipes that use fresh, seasonal ingredients. The flavors, colors and textures work together to create a memorable meal.

COME JOURNEY WITH ME and sample some of the best of Americana such as Down Home Comfort with Kentucky Hot Browns, A Taste of Texas with barbecued brisket and all the trimmings, or a traditional Steak House Dinner. Celebrate special times with Dinner at the Inn, Vineyard Feast, Show-Stopper Dinner, Elegant Spring Dinner or an Appetizer Party. Relax with a casual meal such as Southwest Pleasures with all the robust flavors of the great Southwest or perhaps a Fall Buffet, perfect fare for game day events.

THEN ZIP OFF TO ITALY with me for an incredible Tuscany experience. Although my tender years on the farm are long past, those early memories were revived when I traveled to Tuscany to study with Chef Claudio in his farm kitchen. The rural area, breathtakingly beautiful, will be forever etched in my memory.

THE 27 MENUS IN THIS BOOK are divided into seasons of the year: Spring and Summer, Fall and Winter. Each menu features seasonal foods — fresh, flavorful and usually inexpensive because they are plentiful. For example, a tomato plucked from the garden in July will taste completely different from one purchased from the supermarket in the dead of winter.

COOKING WITH BONNIE: FARM TO FRANCE contains 224 pages of great recipes with tips, make-ahead hints and serving suggestions. Beautiful color photography is displayed throughout the book, making it appealing and easy to use.

How exhilarating to learn from a chef who created authentic Italian dishes from what he produced on his family-owned farm. Now you, too, can experience authentic food from an Italian farm house in the opening chapter: Italian Trattoria Sampler.

JOIN ME IN MY FRENCH ADVENTURE; you will find the journey fascinating and the food outstanding. I received an invitation to teach a cooking class at Atelier Cuisine de Laurence, a French culinary school, in the fall of 2009. Who would have thought a gal who grew up on a small farm in Missouri, picking and shelling bushels of peas from the garden, picking blackberries in the woods while watching for snakes, milking a cow and churning butter would one day be flying off to France to teach the French how to cook American farm food?

AND WHAT DID MY French host request that I teach? American food — Crab Cakes with Remoulade Sauce, Southern Fried Chicken, Mashed Potatoes with Pan Gravy and Blackberry Cobbler. I smiled when I read that — it was traditional farm food that I grew up making. The class was a huge hit — the students loved the food, even gnawing every last morsel of chicken off the bone!

Upper: It was a delight to meet Manuel Martinez, Chef Proprietor of Relais Louis XIII, a famous historical restaurant in Paris. The restaurant is on the very ground where Louis XIII was proclaimed King of France in 1610. Chef Martinez took me back into the kitchen and invited me to work with him, but I had to travel on. Someday soon I hope to return!

Middle: My traveling companions (Rosemary Bartel, Bonnie, Bev Swisher, Lora Palmer, Frank and Sally O'Donnell) on Chef Claudio's farm with the beautiful Tuscan countryside in the background. Working with Chef Claudio in his rural Italian farmhouse is described in *Italian Trattoria Sampler* on page 16.

The pan gravy was a very different kind of sauce for them. Just goes to show that good food knows no boundaries!

MY STORY is one that even I can hardly believe. I am deeply humbled and appreciative of the opportunities I have been given on my culinary journey, the people I have met and the myriad of friends who have enriched my life. Food brings people together — families, friends and perhaps even strangers who grow into friends.

I INVITE YOU to cook with me through the seasons and enjoy your own exciting journey as you savor *Cooking with Bonnie: Farm to France.*

Bonnie

Upper: In Paris, bakeries appeared on nearly every block with windows filled with gorgeous pastries, each beautifully decorated and displayed. I was captivated by the beautiful pastel colors and unusual flavor combinations of the delectable French macaroons.

Lower: Shopping at E. Dehillerin in Paris was an experience to remember! A family owned culinary business since 1820, the shop houses thousands of items stacked high on old wooden shelves and is the very store Julia Child shopped while in Paris.

Italian
TRATTORIA
SAMPLER

Tuscany—just remembering my culinary vacation in Tuscany brings a smile. Though the trip was not what I had expected, it could not have been more perfect. Life has a way of altering one's direction. In 2005, I found myself a widow after a long marriage; my day job of teaching high school had lost its luster. It was time for a change. I quit my job and gave myself a fabulous retirement gift—a culinary vacation to Tuscany. As some of my friends learned of my plans, suddenly they wanted to join me.

The six of us (photo p. 14) arrived at a very old, historic villa, circa 1650, that had been renovated yet surrounded by beautiful, ancient gardens. Chef Claudio, our instructor, spoke English and our classes were taught at his farm house. It sounded so beautifully quaint in the brochure, but it was far more rustic than I could have imagined. What was lacking in equipment, supplies and sanitation, however, was richly compensated by learning how things are actually done in rural areas of Italy. We cooked a chicken from the Chef's farm; only the feathers had been removed. And it had been stored in a dilapidated, plastic dishpan with deep scratches and a huge gash—no shiny, stainless steel pans in sight! We cooked beautiful spinach that went straight from the garden into a pot and ended up as delicious spinach flans. We used eggs that had never been refrigerated, that were whipped up raw and folded into a rich, decadent tiramisu. Eating that way in the States, I am sure we all would have died—perhaps from the fear of it. Not wanting to be Ugly Americans, however, we all enjoyed our new way of eating. Perhaps it was the wine that accompanied the food, but none of us even had a tummy ache.

Looking back, had the kitchen been squeaky clean with an abundance of clean dish towels and aprons every day, had the larvae on the spinach been washed off, had the chicken been cleaned by American standards, and had we not consumed raw eggs, what would we have learned? Yes, we got our money's worth on that trip—the experience was priceless!

I loved Italy - the people, the scenery, the art, and, of course, the food and wine. One evening we ate in an Italian farmhouse next to a winery and the food was fabulous. Now you can experience vicariously the feel and flair of dining in the Tuscan countryside with this menu. Each part of the menu would be great by itself—but together, it is fabulous.

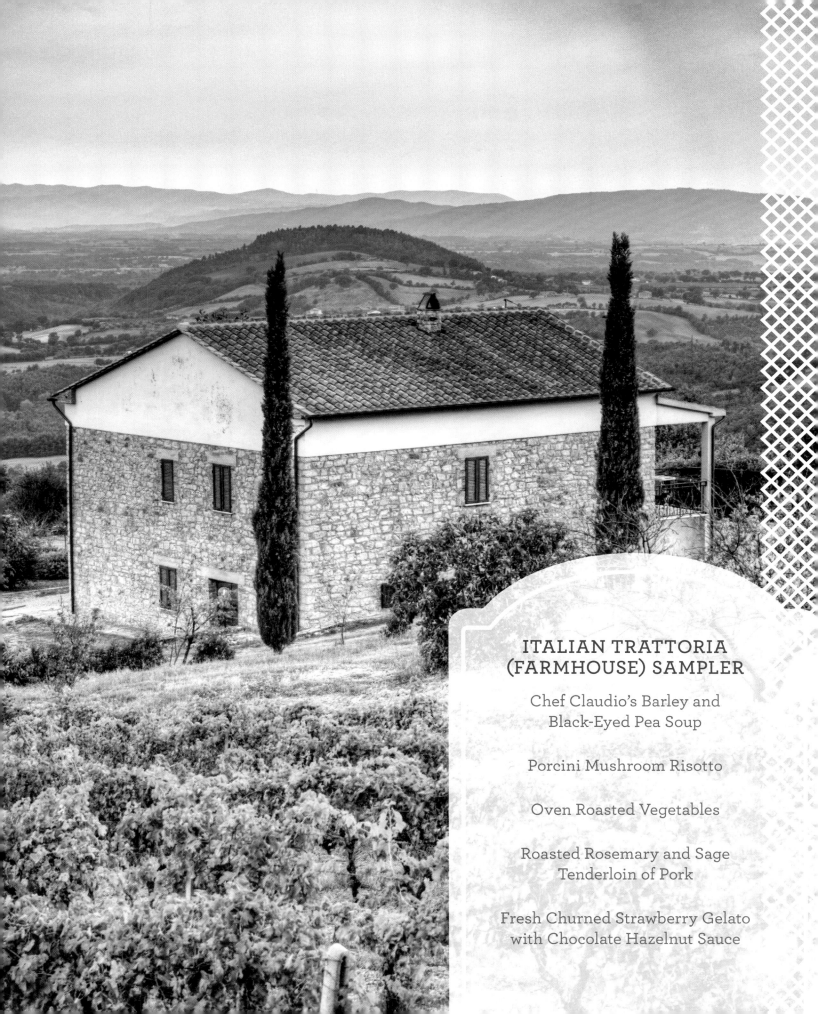

ITALIAN TRATTORIA
(FARMHOUSE) SAMPLER

Chef Claudio's Barley and
Black-Eyed Pea Soup

Porcini Mushroom Risotto

Oven Roasted Vegetables

Roasted Rosemary and Sage
Tenderloin of Pork

Fresh Churned Strawberry Gelato
with Chocolate Hazelnut Sauce

CHEF CLAUDIO'S BARLEY AND BLACK-EYED PEA SOUP

Chef Claudio used lots of beans in his cooking. What we call black-eyed peas, he called black-eyed susan beans, but they are the same. I always assumed black-eyed peas were a U.S. Southern specialty, but they are also enjoyed in Tuscany. This is a great one to make ahead. The flavors blend beautifully and it tastes better the second or third day. The recipe can easily be doubled and part of it frozen for later use.

George Washington Carver promoted the planting of black-eyed peas, a legume, because they add nitrogen to the soil. Throughout the Southern U.S., the black-eyed pea is still widely used as an ingredient. Eating black-eyed peas on New Year's Day is thought to bring prosperity.

¼ cup olive oil
1 medium onion, chopped
1 celery rib, chopped
1 carrot, chopped
1 cup black-eyed peas, picked over, washed and drained
1 bay leaf
2 fresh sage leaves (or ½ teaspoon rubbed dry sage)
1 sprig fresh rosemary
4 (14½-ounce) cans chicken broth
1 cup pearl barley (not quick-cooking)
2 tablespoons tomato paste
Salt and pepper
¼ cup chopped fresh Italian parsley or basil
Garnish: about 3 tablespoons extra virgin olive oil

1. Place oil, onion, celery and carrot in a large stockpot. Cook over medium heat until softened. Add black-eyed peas, bay leaf, sage, rosemary and chicken broth. Bring to a boil; cover and reduce heat and simmer over very low heat for 30 minutes. Add barley and continue to cook 30 to 45 minutes or until black-eyed peas and barley are tender. Remove rosemary sprig.

2. Stir in tomato paste. Season to taste with salt and pepper. Stir in chopped parsley or basil.

3. Ladle into bowls and garnish with a drizzle of olive oil. Makes 6 (1-cup) servings

PORCINI MUSHROOM RISOTTO

This is risotto at its best: bursting with flavors of mushrooms, herbs and Parmesan cheese. Fresh porcini and dried porcini mushrooms are used extensively in Tuscany and they have a strong, earthy flavor. Dried ones must be soaked in boiling water, but reserve the water and use it to add flavor to the dish.

2 (14½-ounce) cans chicken broth
2 tablespoons butter
2 tablespoons olive oil
1 small sweet onion (such as Vidalia or Walla Walla), chopped
12 ounces fresh button mushrooms, cleaned and thinly sliced

¾ ounce dried porcini mushrooms, reconstituted in 1¾ cups boiling water
1 cup Arborio rice or medium-grain rice
½ cup dry sherry
½ cup grated Parmesan cheese
¼ cup thinly sliced green onions
2 teaspoons chopped fresh thyme

1. Bring chicken broth to a simmer in medium saucepan. Reduce heat; keep warm.

2. Combine butter and olive oil in large saucepan; add onion and cook 1 minute. Add fresh mushrooms and cook until tender, about 3 to 4 minutes.

3. Remove dried mushrooms from water, reserve water. Chop mushrooms and add to the pan; cook 2 minutes.

4. Add rice to saucepan, stir to coat. Add sherry and simmer until liquid is absorbed, stirring often.

5. Strain mushroom water and add to the rice. Bring to a boil; reduce heat and simmer until absorbed, stirring frequently. Add chicken broth ¾ cup at a time, allowing broth to be absorbed before adding more; stirring often until rice is just tender and mixture is creamy, about 20 minutes.

6. Stir in Parmesan cheese, green onions and thyme. Serve warm. Makes 6 servings

Porcini mushrooms are most often found in the dried form in large grocery stores in the U.S.; it's less common to find fresh porcini mushrooms here.

Porcini means "piglets" in Italian and is thought to have originated because pigs love devouring porcini mushrooms.

Bonnie's Tip:
When roasting vegetables, be sure they are only one layer thick so they will actually roast and develop rich caramelized edges that contribute to the flavor of the dish.

If piled in a pan a few layers deep, they will end up steaming instead of roasting; still good but not quite the same.

OVEN ROASTED VEGETABLES

Chef Claudio grew most of his own vegetables. We used zucchini in multiple dishes and even stuffed and fried zucchini blossoms. We must have made a minimum of three zucchini dishes each day - it was very plentiful!

1 eggplant, peeled and sliced ½ inch thick, then cut into cubes
2 carrots, thinly sliced
1 large sweet onion (such as a Vidalia or Walla Walla), cut into 10 wedges
3 medium green zucchini, sliced ⅓ inch thick on diagonal
2 yellow summer squash, sliced ⅓ inch thick on diagonal

2 red bell peppers, cored and seeded, and cut into strips
2 tablespoons chopped fresh basil (or 1½ teaspoons dried leaf basil)
2 teaspoons minced garlic
3 to 4 tablespoons olive oil
¼ cup grated Parmesan cheese
1 teaspoon kosher salt to taste
½ teaspoon freshly ground black pepper

1. Preheat oven to 425°F. Place vegetables in a large bowl and toss with basil, garlic, olive oil, Parmesan cheese, salt and pepper.

2. Spread vegetables in a single layer on a large rimmed baking sheet. Bake until vegetable edges are golden brown, stirring occasionally, about 30 minutes. Taste and add additional salt and pepper, if desired. Serve warm. Makes 10 side-dish servings

ROASTED ROSEMARY AND SAGE TENDERLOIN OF PORK

The tenderloins may be rubbed with the herbs and roasted immediately, but for best flavor rub them with the herb mixture, place in a large zipper-lock bag and refrigerate 4 to 24 hours before roasting.

2 large garlic cloves, pressed
1 tablespoon olive oil
1 teaspoon dried rubbed sage
2 teaspoons chopped fresh rosemary (or 1 teaspoon dried rosemary)
¾ teaspoon kosher salt

¼ teaspoon ground black pepper
2 pork tenderloins (about 1 pound each)
½ cup white wine or chicken broth
1 tablespoon butter, optional
Garnish: Fresh rosemary sprigs (optional)

1. Preheat oven to 450°F. Mix first six ingredients in bowl. Rub garlic-herb mixture all over pork.

2. Place pork in 11-inch skillet or shallow roasting pan. Roast 20 to 25 minutes or until thermometer inserted into center of pork registers 150°F. Remove from oven; let stand 10 minutes. Tenderloins will still be rosy in the center.

3. Remove pork from pan, tent with foil. Deglaze pan with wine or broth. Stir and scrape bottom of pan to dissolve any brown bits that will add flavor to the sauce; bring liquid to a boil. Remove from heat. Stir in a tablespoon of butter if desired. Cut pork crosswise into ⅓-inch-thick-slices. Arrange pork slices on platter. Pour pan juices over. Garnish with rosemary sprigs, if desired. Makes 6 to 8 servings

The tenderloin comes from the full pork loin. As the name indicates, the tenderloin is one of the most tender cuts. Typically, pork tenderloin weighs between ¾ and 1½ pounds.

Pork tenderloin makes an elegant entrée for a small dinner party but also can be roasted or grilled whole for a quick weeknight dinner. When sliced crosswise (like a loaf of French bread), the resulting medallions also may be sautéed.

Pork tenderloin has a mild flavor, so it's best when prepared with an added spice rub, marinade, stuffing or flavorful sauce. To keep the tenderloin juicy, be careful not to overcook.

FRESH CHURNED STRAWBERRY GELATO WITH CHOCOLATE HAZELNUT SAUCE

The gelato was fabulous in Italy and I enjoyed it every day I was there—some days more than one time. My friends and I would select different flavors and then sample each other's. It was impossible to pick a favorite: they all were delicious.

1½ cups whole milk
½ cup heavy cream
1 cup plus 2 tablespoons sugar,
    divided use
3 tablespoons corn syrup, divided use
2 whole eggs
1 pound frozen unsweetened
    strawberries, thawed (or 4 cups fresh)
2 tablespoons fresh lemon juice

Chocolate Hazelnut Sauce
⅓ cup cream
½ cup chocolate hazelnut spread (like
    Nutella)

1. For the Gelato: In a heavy 2-quart saucepan heat milk, cream, 2 tablespoons sugar and 1 tablespoon corn syrup until very hot but not boiling. Meanwhile, beat eggs with electric mixer until light and lemon colored. Temper eggs by whisking about a cup of the hot milk mixture into the eggs; then pour egg mixture into pan. Cook, stirring contantly, until mixture becomes thick and will coat the back of a wooden spoon. Strain into a clean container and cool; refrigerate several hours.

2. Meanwhile, puree strawberries with electric blender or food processor. Stir in lemon juice, 2 tablespoons corn syrup and remaining cup of sugar. Stir berry mixture into chilled cream mixture.

3. Pour cooled mixture into ice cream freezer container and freeze according to manufacturer's instructions. Transfer to freezer container, cover and chill in freezer up to 4 hours to allow flavors to ripen. Makes 1½ quarts

4. For the Sauce: Heat cream in a microwave-safe glass measure for 20 to 30 seconds or until it is very hot. Remove and whisk in Nutella until mixture is smooth. Use immediately; may be stored in refrigerator 2 weeks. Warm gently in microwave before serving. Makes about ½ cup sauce

Bonnie's Tip:
Chill the cream mixture completely before adding the pureed berries. If berries are added to the warm mixture, it is likely to curdle the cream.
It is very easy to make the cream base and the pureed berries a day in advance; chill separately, and then combine when ready to freeze the mixture.

Elegant SPRING DINNER

I dearly love this menu—it is the kind of food that often appeared on our table in the springtime when I was a child growing up in rural Missouri. Ham was smoked and cured over the winter and was ready for cooking in the spring. Fresh asparagus had to be harvested daily; the spears shot up quickly overnight, much like mushrooms. Delicate, peppery watercress grew wild near the natural springs in the Ozarks; here I use it in soup, but it also was often used in salad mixed with the first leaf lettuce from the garden.

I have included two wonderful soups in this menu—you can't go wrong with either. The watercress soup is delicate and delicious but

if watercress is difficult to find, the carrot soup has won rave reviews in my cooking classes. When you cook a ham, expect to enjoy wonderful leftovers; feast on ham sandwiches, use the bone to make a great bean soup and do try the recipe for Hot Ham Canapés with Raspberry Chipotle Sauce found elsewhere in this book. You will want to say as we do in the South, "Come on over and eat with us!" That's one way to make life-long friends!

ELEGANT SPRING DINNER

Cream of Watercress Soup *or*
Cream of Carrot Soup

Orange Glazed Baked Ham

Creamed New Potatoes and Peas

Steamed Asparagus with
Tomato Herb Salsa

Strawberries and Cream Cake

CREAM OF WATERCRESS SOUP

A beautiful spring soup featuring the fresh, piquant flavor of watercress.

⅓ cup butter
1 medium onion, chopped
2 cloves garlic, minced
2 large Idaho potatoes (1 pound) peeled and sliced
½ teaspoon salt
¼ teaspoon ground red pepper

2 bunches (about 8 ounces total) watercress, washed and coarse stems removed
2½ cups chicken broth
2 to 2½ cups half-and-half
½ cup flour
2 tablespoons fresh lemon juice
Pinch freshly grated nutmeg

Watercress is a semi-aquatic plant with a peppery flavor. It can be found in the produce department of large supermarkets. In certain areas, it grows wild near creek banks or natural springs. My mother told the story of picking it wild by the spring where she grew up in southern Missouri.

1. **Melt** butter in a 3-quart saucepan over medium heat. Add onion and garlic; sauté until tender. Add potatoes, salt, pepper and 2 cups water. Bring to a boil; reduce heat and simmer 20 minutes or until potatoes are tender.

2. **Reserve** a few sprigs of watercress for garnish. Coarsely chop remaining watercress and add to potatoes, along with chicken broth. Simmer for 10 minutes.

3. **Pour** 1 cup half-and-half in a blender; add flour. Blend until smooth. Ladle watercress-potato mixture into blender. (Do this in batches so the blender does not overflow.) Blend until mixture is smooth; repeat process until all has been pureed. Return to the saucepan.

4. **Bring** to a boil over medium heat and simmer until thickened. Stir in 1 cup half-and-half. If a thinner consistency is desired, stir in remaining half-and-half. Bring back to a simmer. Season with lemon juice, nutmeg and additional salt and pepper if desired. Ladle into bowls and garnish with watercress sprigs.
Makes 8 (1-cup) servings

CREAM OF CARROT SOUP

This soup has been a cooking class favorite, which always surprises me because it is so simple to make. I have even substituted evaporated skim milk for the cream when I made this for a low-calorie class and it was delicious, too. The soup may be made in advance, cooled and refrigerated. Warm over medium heat before serving.

1 pound carrots, peeled and cut into
   1-inch pieces
1 medium potato, peeled and cubed
½ medium onion, coarsely chopped
1 clove garlic, crushed
2 (14½-ounce) cans chicken broth
1¼ teaspoons dried thyme

½ teaspoon salt
⅛ to ¼ teaspoon ground red pepper
½ to ¾ cup heavy cream (can
   substitute half-and-half or fat-free
   evaporated milk for low-fat version)
Garnish: Chopped chives or scallions

1. Place carrots, potato, onion, garlic, chicken broth, thyme, salt and ground red pepper in a heavy saucepan. Bring to a boil. Reduce heat and simmer for 20 to 25 minutes or until vegetables are very tender.

2. Puree in batches in blender or food processor. (If using a blender, remember hot mixtures have a tendency to "explode" so fill blender only about two-thirds full. Remove

cover of small opening on top of blender and place a towel over it and then blend. The towel will allow steam to escape while keeping the carrot mixture inside the blender and not on your ceiling!)

3. Return pureed mixture to pan. Gradually stir in cream. Taste and adjust salt and pepper, if desired. Serve warm garnished with chopped chives or scallions. Makes about 6 (1-cup) servings

Evaporated milk is canned, pasteurized milk. Once it is reconstituted with an equal part water, it has the same qualities as fresh milk. It does have a darker color and a cooked taste due to the processing. However, when cooked, it is not detectable.

ORANGE GLAZED BAKED HAM

Be sure to use a good quality ham. The label should read "ham and natural juices." Those marked "ham and water product" may look like a bargain, but can contain up to 23 percent water. The texture and flavor of those are not like the real thing and they will shrink substantially during cooking as the water escapes.

1 (8 to 10 pound) smoked, fully cooked
    bone-in, half ham (such as Hillshire or
    Hormel 81)

Glaze
½ cup orange marmalade
¼ cup Dijon mustard
¼ cup brown sugar, firmly packed
Garnish: fresh herbs, lemon leaves or
    orange slices (optional)

Bonnie's Tip:
Try to find a ham that is not spiral cut. They have a better appearance, are generally more moist and, frankly, I like to cut my own slices.

1. Position rack in center of oven and preheat to 325°F. Place ham in roasting pan and cook according to package directions or until internal temperature is 150°F.

2. Meanwhile, bring orange marmalade, mustard and brown sugar to a boil in a small saucepan. Set aside.

3. Thirty minutes before ham is done, remove from oven and brush with glaze. Return to oven to finish cooking, allowing for glaze to set and caramelization to begin. Let ham stand 30 minutes before slicing. Garnish with fresh herbs, lemon leaves and orange slices.

CREAMED NEW POTATOES AND PEAS

Growing up on a farm, my dad always planted a huge garden and his goal was to get it planted early! We almost always had a mess of fresh peas and fresh-dug potatoes by Memorial Day, cooked together and finished with heavy cream. Talk about good! Here we are using frozen peas. However, if you are lucky enough to get fresh ones, by all means use them.

2 pounds small, new red potatoes
½ teaspoon salt
1 (16-ounce) bag frozen baby peas
1 teaspoon sugar, optional
¾ to 1 cup heavy cream
Salt and freshly ground black pepper to taste

1. Scrub potatoes. Peel a strip from around the equator of each potato. Place potatoes, 1 cup water and ½ teaspoon salt in a large saucepan. Bring to a boil. Reduce heat, cover and simmer until tender, about 20 minutes.

2. Add frozen peas and sugar to potatoes; cover and cook for 3 or 4 minutes. There will not be much liquid left in the pan. Remove lid and cook a few minutes to evaporate most of liquid. Add cream and simmer uncovered a few minutes until cream is thickened to sauce consistency. Season to taste with salt and freshly ground black pepper. Makes 8 servings

Bonnie's Tip:
You must use new potatoes because the flavor is delicate and sweeter. To see if your potatoes are new, scratch the potato a few times with your fingernail. If the peel is easily removed, you have a new potato.

STEAMED ASPARAGUS WITH TOMATO HERB SALSA

This is a beautiful dish to make when asparagus is in peak season. The colorful ribbon of Tomato Herb Salsa is a delightful flavor combination with the asparagus.

Tomato Herb Salsa
2 cups diced, seeded tomatoes
½ cup thinly sliced green onion
¼ cup chopped fresh basil
3 tablespoons extra virgin olive oil
1 tablespoon white wine or balsamic
　vinegar
Salt and freshly ground black pepper to
　taste

2 pounds fresh asparagus, tough ends
　snapped off
½ teaspoon salt
¼ cup butter
1 tablespoon fresh lemon juice
2 tablespoons chopped fresh parsley
Salt and freshly ground pepper to taste

1. For the Tomato Herb Salsa: Combine all ingredients together in a bowl. Season with salt and pepper. Cover and set aside for flavors to blend while asparagus cooks.

2. For the asparagus: Place 1 cup water and ½ teaspoon salt in a deep pan. Insert steamer basket. Place asparagus in basket, stem ends down. Bring to a boil; reduce heat to a simmer. Cover and steam for 7 to 10 minutes until tender crisp. Remove from steamer basket. Drain and arrange on large platter.

3. To serve: Melt butter; stir in lemon juice and parsley. Drizzle over asparagus. Sprinkle with salt and freshly ground black pepper. Spoon a ribbon of Tomato Herb Salsa over asparagus and serve. Makes 6 to 8 servings

Bonnie's Tip:
If advance preparation is desired, steam asparagus then immediately plunge in ice water to stop the cooking and to set the color. Drain. Place in covered container and refrigerate up to 24 hours. Before serving, place on microwave platter and reheat; or dip in boiling water for 30 seconds. Drain and proceed.

Strawberries and Cream Cake, p. 31

STRAWBERRIES AND CREAM CAKE

A delicate butter cake with a moist crumb, layered with whipped crème fraîche and sliced strawberries. Tastes as good as it looks!

Cake
3 large eggs
1 cup milk, divided use
2 teaspoons vanilla extract
½ teaspoon almond extract
½ teaspoon grated lemon zest
3 cups sifted cake flour
1½ cups sugar
1 tablespoon plus 1 teaspoon baking
    powder
¾ teaspoon salt
¾ cup (1½ sticks) unsalted butter
    room temperature

1 quart strawberries
2 tablespoons sugar
1 tablespoon strawberry jelly, optional

Whipped Crème Fraîche
3 cups chilled heavy cream
½ cup chilled sour cream
¾ cup powdered sugar
1 teaspoon vanilla extract

1. **Preheat** oven to 350°F. Grease and flour two 9-inch cake pans. Set aside.

2. **Combine** eggs, ¼ cup milk, vanilla extract, almond extract and lemon zest in a small bowl.

3. **In large mixer bowl,** combine cake flour, sugar, baking powder and salt. Mix on low for 30 seconds to combine ingredients. Add butter and remaining ¾ cup milk; mix on low to blend, then turn mixer to medium and beat 2 minutes. Scrape down sides.

4. **Gradually** add egg mixture in three batches, beating well after each addition and scraping down sides as needed.

5. **Divide** batter between prepared pans and smooth surface. Bake 25 to 35 minutes or until a wooden skewer inserted near the center comes out clean and the cake springs back when lightly pressed near the center. Remove from oven; cool on rack for 10 minutes. Remove cakes from pans; cool completely.

6. **Meanwhile,** rinse and cap strawberries. Reserve about half of the most beautiful and uniform-sized ones for the top of the cake. Slice the remaining berries. Sprinkle with 2 tablespoons sugar. Let stand at room temperature 20 to 30 minutes for juices to accumulate.

7. **To make the Whipped Crème Fraîche:** Using electric mixer, beat cream, sour cream, powdered sugar and vanilla until stiff peaks form.

8. **To assemble the cake:** Place one cake layer on platter. Spread with a thin layer of Whipped Crème Fraîche. Top with a layer of sliced, sweetened strawberries. Spread with a layer of Whipped Crème Fraîche. Top with second cake layer, pressing lightly. Spread remaining Whipped Crème Fraîche over sides and top of cake, forming a ridge along the top edges of the cake. Slice the reserved berries and fill in the top of the cake with strawberries. Brush berries with melted strawberry jelly if desired. Cover cake with dome and refrigerate. May be made a day in advance of serving.

Cake flour is a silky, low protein flour used for baking delicate cakes. Two popular national brands are Softasilk and Swans Down.

Bonnie's Tip:
The sour cream folded into the whipped cream frosting adds a delightful flavor but also serves as a stabilizer. The whipped cream will remain firm and holds quite nicely. However, remember to keep the cake refrigerated.

TIME *to* CELEBRATE

Graduations, engagements, weddings or simply
the wonders of spring—all are good reasons to celebrate!
I have made this menu numerous times to commemorate
special occasions. The entrée is a showstopper: fresh salmon,
butterflied and filled with a savory spinach stuffing. This
dessert will have your guests gasping in
amazement. Your little secret will be how
easy it was to make!

I could have named this menu
"Four Star Menu" because it is just
that beautiful and delicious. The most
challenging part is the salmon roulade,
but take it a step at a time and you will be
amazed at how easily it comes together.
The side dishes require little effort, and
the orzo will likely be your new favorite—
it's just that good!

TIME TO CELEBRATE

Artichoke and Roasted
Pepper Tapenade

Tossed Green Salad with
Orange Vinaigrette

Roasted Salmon Roulade
with Spinach Feta Filling

Orzo Parmesan with Basil,
Scallions and Peppers

Fresh Green Beans Almondine

Blackberry Rippled Baked Alaska

ARTICHOKE AND ROASTED PEPPER TAPENADE

Tapenade is a dish that originated in the Mediterranean and traditionally consists of olives and capers. This rendition incorporates artichokes and other ingredients to make a very tasty spread.

1 garlic clove
¾ cup loosely packed fresh parsley, rinsed, dried and stems removed
1 (6½-ounce) jar marinated artichoke hearts, drained
⅓ cup Mediterranean-style olives, pitted
⅓ cup jarred, roasted red peppers, rinsed and drained
⅓ cup grated Parmesan cheese

⅓ cup extra virgin olive oil
⅓ cup walnuts or almonds toasted
1 tablespoon lemon juice
1 teaspoon capers
¼ teaspoon dried leaf thyme
¼ teaspoon dried leaf oregano
Pinch ground red pepper
Salt and pepper
Baguette slices

Capers are buds of a bush that is native to the Mediterranean region. The buds are harvested and pickled in a brine and are used frequently in Mediterranean cuisine.

1. Fit food processor with metal blade and with machine running, drop garlic clove through the feed tube. Process until chopped. Add parsley and process until finely chopped.

2. Add artichokes, olives, roasted red peppers, Parmesan cheese, olive oil, walnuts, lemon juice, capers, thyme, oregano and red pepper to food processor. Pulse (on/off motions) until mixture is coarsely chopped. Taste; season to taste with salt and pepper. May be made 24 hours in advance, covered and chilled. Serve with baguette slices. Makes 1¾ cups

TOSSED GREEN SALAD WITH ORANGE VINAIGRETTE

I have made this salad numerous times in cooking classes and it is always a favorite. The Orange Vinaigrette is fresh and inviting. When fresh oranges are in season, I often section them to make the salad really special. Mandarin oranges are a great substitute; I have never had any complaints.

12 cups assorted, washed greens
(spinach, romaine and/or mixed baby
lettuce)
1 (12-ounce) can mandarin oranges,
drained
½ small red onion, cut into thin wedges
and separated
Garnish: Sliced almonds, slightly toasted

Orange Vinaigrette
1 tablespoon Dijon mustard
2 tablespoons orange juice concentrate
⅓ cup rice vinegar
1½ teaspoons grated orange rind,
optional
¾ teaspoon salt
⅛ teaspoon ground red pepper
1 tablespoon honey
¾ cup vegetable oil
¼ cup thinly sliced green onions or
fresh chives
⅓ cup toasted sliced almonds

1. Tear well-washed greens into bite size pieces. Place in a large bowl with oranges and red onion.

2. Place mustard, orange juice concentrate, rice vinegar, grated orange rind, salt, ground red pepper and honey in bowl of food processor fitted with metal blade or blender. Process until mixed. Gradually add vegetable oil in a thin stream while machine is running, adding enough to make a thin emulsion. Add chives and almonds. Process only 3 or 4 seconds to mix.

3. Cover and chill dressing until ready to use. Before using, stir and pour over chilled dry greens. Toss to coat. Divide salad among plates. Garnish each with almonds.
Makes 8 to 10 servings

Bonnie's Tip:
To toast almonds, place them on a shallow rimmed baking sheet. Toast in a preheated 350°F oven for 8 to 12 minutes or until golden and fragrant. Watch carefully, because they will go from "toasted" to "burnt" very quickly.

FRESH GREEN BEANS ALMONDINE

3 tablespoons butter
⅓ cup sliced almonds
1 teaspoon sugar
1½ pounds fresh green beans, ends and strings removed
Salt and pepper

1. Melt butter in a large skillet over medium heat. Add almonds and sauté until lightly browned. Stir in sugar. Remove from heat and set aside.

2. Rinse green beans and break into 2 inch pieces. Steam green beans 7 to 10 minutes or until tender. Length of time will depend upon the maturity of the green beans. Drain and toss with almond butter mixture. Season with salt and pepper and serve. Makes 6 servings

ORZO PARMESAN WITH BASIL, SCALLIONS AND PEPPERS

Bonnie's Tip:
Cold temperature will cause basil leaves to darken—that is why basil grown outside will turn dark in the fall even before frost. The cooler night temperatures will darken the leaves.

Once washed, wrap fresh basil in paper towels to wick the water away from the tender leaves, place in a plastic bag and store in a warmer part of the refrigerator.

Orzo is a small, rice-shaped pasta. However, the first time I cooked it many years ago, I did not realize that. It looked like rice, so I cooked it like rice and one of my best recipes was created. I have made variations of this for a long time and it is always a favorite. Use fresh basil in this recipe, as that truly is the secret of its flavor. If I can't get fresh basil, I don't even bother making this.

3 tablespoons butter
1 pound orzo (rice shaped pasta)
2 (14½-ounce) cans chicken broth
  (prefer Swanson's)
½ cup water
½ cup frozen baby peas
2 tablespoons small diced red bell pepper

½ cup freshly grated Parmesan cheese
⅓ cup chopped fresh basil
¼ cup chopped fresh chives or scallions
Salt and freshly ground black pepper
Garnish: Fresh basil

1. **Melt** butter in heavy saucepan. Add orzo and sauté 2 minutes.

2. **Add** chicken broth and ½ cup water; bring to a boil. Reduce heat; simmer, uncovered, until orzo is tender and liquid is almost absorbed, about 7 to 8 minutes.

3. **Stir** in peas and red bell pepper. Remove from heat and cover tightly and let stand for 1 to 2 minutes. Stir in Parmesan cheese, basil and chives. Taste and add salt and pepper if needed. Garnish with fresh basil before serving. Makes 8 servings

Roasted Salmon Roulade with Spinach Feta Filling, p. 37

ROASTED SALMON ROULADE WITH SPINACH FETA FILLING

My friend Jill Koehn was the inspiration for this recipe. Jill described to me in great detail a salmon roulade she enjoyed while on vacation. I took the idea and this is my rendition. It may seem very involved, but each step is easy to accomplish. The roulade is made a day in advance of serving, which is always a benefit when entertaining.

Filling
1 tablespoon olive oil
½ cup chopped onion
1 garlic clove, minced
16 ounces fresh baby spinach, blanched, refreshed and pressed to remove excess water (or 1 [10-ounce] package frozen, chopped spinach, thawed and well drained)
¾ cup ricotta cheese (regular or reduced fat)
¼ cup sour cream (regular or reduced fat)
½ cup (4 ounces) crumbled feta cheese
¼ cup freshly grated Parmesan cheese
1 tablespoon fresh lemon juice
1 teaspoon dried thyme leaves
¾ teaspoon salt
¼ teaspoon crushed red pepper
⅛ teaspoon nutmeg

Side of fresh salmon, approximately 2½ to 3 pounds, skin removed
Kosher salt
Lemon pepper

Crumb Coating
3 cups fresh bread crumbs
3 tablespoons butter, melted
Lemon pepper
¾ teaspoon dried dill weed (or 1 tablespoon chopped fresh dill)
Garnish: Lemon twists, fresh dill (optional)

Bonnie's Tip:
To make fresh bread crumbs, tear a few slices of bread and place in bowl of food processor fitted with the metal blade.

Turn on and process until bread is broken down into crumbs. You can also make bread crumbs in a blender, but process only one slice at a time. Day old bread makes the best crumbs.

1. For the Spinach Filling: Heat olive oil in skillet over medium heat. Sauté onion and garlic for a minute or two until softened - do not brown garlic. Remove from heat. Stir in rest of filling ingredients. Set aside.

2. For the Salmon: Place salmon on a large cutting board. Trim off any dark colored flesh on side which was next to the skin; discard. Looking at the side of salmon, you will see an area where it begins to get thick. Beginning at that point, butterfly salmon lengthwise, being careful not to cut all the way through. Open up the salmon (like a book) and you will have a thin, double-width filet of salmon. Cut a piece of wide, heavy-duty aluminum foil about 10 inches longer than the salmon. Then place a piece of parchment paper on top of the foil. Carefully place the salmon on the parchment paper.

3. Season salmon with salt and lemon pepper. Spread the filling over the entire surface except for about an inch strip along one of the long sides. To make the roulade, start with the long side toward you and roll up, jellyroll fashion.

4. Combine bread crumbs, butter, lemon pepper and dill weed. Press crumb mixture over surface of roulade. To finish, roll the parchment-foil around the salmon roulade, twist the ends together tightly. Chill at least for 1 hour and up to 24 hours to firm the roll.

5. Preheat oven to 450°F. Unwrap salmon and slice into 1-inch slices. Transfer slices to a lightly oiled, foil-lined baking sheet. Cook for 10 minutes or until fish flakes. Garnish as desired. Makes about 10 servings

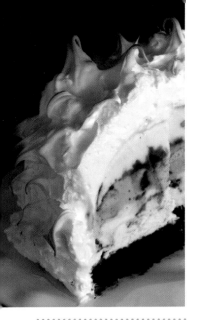

BLACKBERRY RIPPLED BAKED ALASKA

When you make this, expect applause. It is stunning, but not difficult to make. Just take each part of the recipe and do it in segments.

Filling
3 cups strawberry ice cream, softened
3 cups vanilla ice cream, softened
3 cups butter-pecan ice cream, softened
1 cup Blackberry Sauce (recipe follows)

Meringue
1 cup egg whites (about 8 large
   egg whites)
Pinch salt
½ teaspoon cream of tartar
1 cup sugar

Brownie base
4 ounces fine-quality bittersweet
   chocolate chips
½ cup (1 stick) butter
¾ cup sugar
3 large eggs
⅛ teaspoon salt
½ cup unsweetened cocoa powder

Bonnie's Tip:
Construct this recipe in parts so it does not overwhelm you. Make the brownie base, make the berry sauce, and make the layered ice cream mound all in advance. Then assemble it, spread on the meringue, and pop it in the freezer. When totally frozen, wrap in plastic wrap; it will hold well for one week in the freezer.

1. For the Filling: Line a 2 ½-quart bowl that is 9-inches in diameter with plastic wrap so that the wrap comes over the sides of the bowl. Spread strawberry ice cream evenly into the bottom of the bowl. Drizzle with one-third of the blackberry sauce. Top with vanilla ice cream; drizzle with one-third blackberry sauce; top with butter-pecan ice cream and drizzle with remaining blackberry sauce. Smooth the top. Cover the ice cream and bowl with plastic wrap. Place in freezer until hardened, at least 8 hours, or overnight.

2. For the Brownie Base: Preheat oven to 375°F. Line a 9-inch round cake pan with a 12-inch circle of parchment paper. Lightly spray with a pan release product.

3. Place chocolate and butter in a glass container and microwave on Medium for 30 to 45 seconds or until butter is melted. Place in a mixing bowl with sugar, whisking to mix well. Whisk in eggs and salt, then add cocoa and stir until just combined.

4. Spread batter evenly into pan. Bake on middle rack until tester comes out with only a few crumbs adhering, about 25 to 35 minutes. Cool brownie completely; turn pan upside down on flat surface and lift pan off brownie. Peel off parchment. Let cool completely.

5. To assemble: Open the plastic wrap covering the ice cream so that the ice cream is exposed. Place the brownie directly on top of the ice cream. Press down slightly so it adheres. Wrap plastic over top of brownie and return to freezer for another 30 minutes or longer.

6. Beat egg whites, a pinch of salt and cream of tartar with an electric mixer and continue to beat until whites hold soft peaks. Gradually add the sugar while beating, and continue beating until whites just hold stiff, glossy peaks.

7. Remove ice cream base from freezer and invert on an oven-safe platter or sheet pan. (You may need to briefly dip it into a bowl with hot water to loosen it, being careful not to get any water into the bowl.)

Spread the meringue evenly over the dessert in a swirling motion or pipe decoratively. Return to the freezer for at least 3 hours or up to two days. After meringue has frozen, wrap in plastic wrap.

8. When ready to serve, heat the oven to 500°F. Remove the dessert from the freezer, unwrap and place it in the oven. Bake 3 to 4 minutes or until browned. Serve slices with blackberry sauce if desired. Makes 8 to 10 servings

BLACKBERRY SAUCE

1 (12-ounce) bag frozen, unsweetened blackberries, thawed
1 teaspoon lemon juice
½ cup sugar

1. Place thawed berries, lemon juice and sugar in blender. Process to blend. Pour through a strainer to remove seeds. You may need to push the seeds and pulp with a spatula to work all the juice through the strainer. Store sauce in a covered container in the refrigerator. It will keep 7 days.

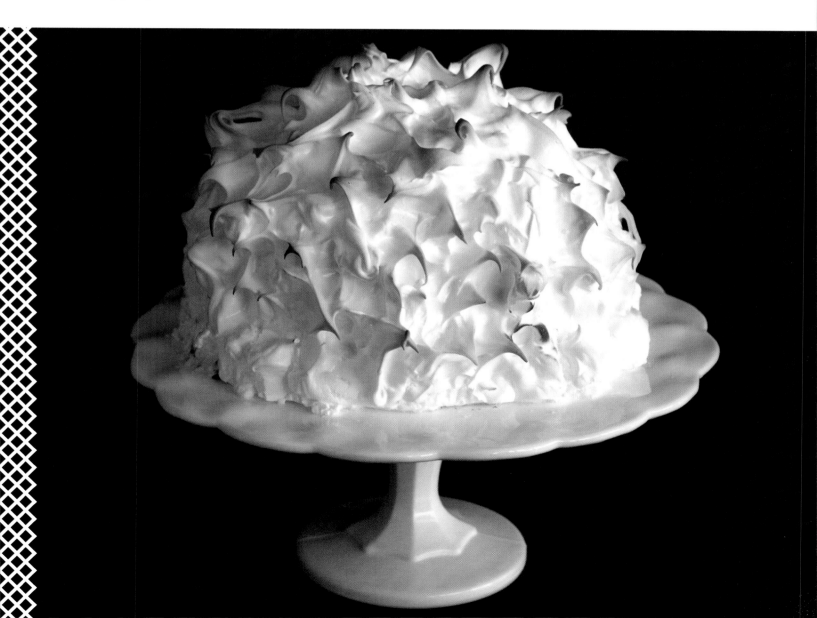

FLORIDA'S *Treasure Coast* CUISINE

While vacationing on Florida's Treasure Coast, I had lunch at a tiki bar and the salad made an indelible memory—it was crisp, fresh and topped with the most magnificent crunchy Key West shrimp. They were pink, plump, succulent gems. As I sampled food along the Treasure Coast, I enjoyed the flavors, the combinations and even the vibrant colors and could not wait to get home to recreate some of the foods I enjoyed while there.

This menu has a special significance to me as well—it was the first class I taught when I opened *Cooking at Bonnie's Place*, a

cooking school and retail store in Wichita, Kansas. My son Eddie flew in from Florida and my daughter Christy came from Kansas City to attend my first class in the new store, making it a very special event.

This fabulous menu is packed with rich cultural flavors of Florida's Treasure Coast— Latino, Cuban and Caribbean intertwined with many agricultural products produced in the Sunshine State. This has been a cooking class I have repeated often because of its popularity. One woman came the first time it was offered, then brought a friend the second time because she liked the food so much!

FLORIDA'S TREASURE COAST CUISINE

Tiki Bar Salad with Panko-Crusted
Key West Shrimp

Sweet and Spicy Glazed
Pork Tenderloin

Cuban Black Beans with Tomato Salsa

Coconut Cilantro Rice

Key Lime Tart in Coconut Crust

TIKI BAR SALAD WITH PANKO-CRUSTED KEY WEST SHRIMP

A great salad to start a meal, or increase serving size and make it a main course!

Bonnie's Tip:
Panko crumbs, also known as Japanese bread crumbs, can be found in most supermarkets. They are coarser and crunchier than regular bread crumbs.

Bonnie's Tip:
It is important to not overcook shrimp. Shrimp cooks very quickly and you can tell when it is done because it will curl and the color changes from translucent to opaque. If in doubt, cut a shrimp in half. If opaque, or milky white on the interior, it is done.

Lime Vinaigrette
¼ cup fresh lime juice
1 tablespoon Dijon mustard
1 tablespoon orange marmalade
1 tablespoon honey
½ cup vegetable oil
2 tablespoons chopped cilantro
½ teaspoon salt
¼ teaspoon black pepper

Salad
8 cups mixed greens (prefer spring
   greens and romaine)
1 red bell pepper, chopped
1 cup frozen corn kernels, thawed
1 avocado, sliced

Shrimp
¾ pound medium wild-caught shrimp,
   peeled and deveined
1 teaspoon lemon pepper
¾ teaspoon Jamaican jerk seasoning
1 cup flour seasoned with 1 teaspoon salt
   and ¼ teaspoon black pepper
2 eggs beaten with 2 tablespoons milk
1½ cups panko crumbs seasoned with 1
   teaspoon salt and ¼ teaspoon ground
   red pepper
Vegetable oil for frying

1. For the Lime Vinaigrette: Whisk lime juice and Dijon mustard together in a small, deep bowl. Stir in orange marmalade and honey. Gradually whisk in oil until mixture thickens. Stir in cilantro, salt and pepper.

2. For the Shrimp: Shrimp may be pan-fried or deep-fried. Preheat oil in deep skillet or deep fryer to 360°F. Rinse shrimp and pat dry. Season with lemon pepper and Jamaican jerk seasoning. Dredge shrimp in the seasoned flour, shaking off any excess. Dip the shrimp in the egg wash and then in the seasoned panko crumbs. Fry until golden brown and cooked through. Drain on paper towels.

3. To assemble the Salad: Combine salad ingredients in a large bowl. Add enough dressing to coat greens. Arrange panko-crusted shrimp over top of salad. Drizzle with additional dressing if desired. Makes 6 servings

SWEET AND SPICY GLAZED PORK TENDERLOIN

Wonderful flavors in this tenderloin! Once the tenderloins are browned in the skillet, just place the skillet with the browned meat into the oven to finish cooking.

Pork Tenderloin
2 teaspoons salt
½ teaspoon black pepper
1 teaspoon smoked paprika
¾ teaspoon ground cumin
¾ teaspoon chili powder
¾ teaspoon cinnamon
2 pork tenderloins (2¼ to 2½ pounds total)
2 tablespoons olive oil

Glaze
1 cup dark brown sugar, firmly packed
1 tablespoon Dijon mustard
1 garlic clove, minced
¼ teaspoon ground red pepper

Smoked paprika is made from peppers that are dried slowly over an oak burning fire for several weeks. The result is a sweet, cool, smoky flavor. This spice is a great way to add a smoky flavor with no heat.

1. Preheat oven to 350°F. Stir together salt, pepper, paprika, cumin, chili powder and cinnamon, then coat pork with spice rub.

2. Heat oil in an ovenproof 12-inch heavy skillet over moderately high heat until just beginning to smoke, then brown pork, turning, about 4 minutes total.

3. Make the glaze by stirring together brown sugar, Dijon mustard, garlic and ground red pepper; pat on top of each tenderloin.

4. Roast in middle of oven until thermometer inserted diagonally in center of each tenderloin registers 150°F, about 20 minutes. Let pork stand in skillet at room temperature for 10 minutes. (Temperature will rise to about 155°F while standing.) Slice and serve.
Makes 6 to 8 servings

CUBAN BLACK BEANS WITH TOMATO SALSA

This dish, loaded with Latin flavors, has been a cooking class favorite. In addition to its spectacular flavors, with the contrasting colors it also plates beautifully.

2 tablespoons olive oil
1 red (or yellow or orange) bell pepper, cut into thin short strips
½ cup chopped onion
2 cloves garlic minced
2 (16-ounce) cans black beans, drained and rinsed
2 tablespoons white wine vinegar
¼ teaspoon ground red pepper
3 to 4 tablespoons minced fresh cilantro
Salt and freshly ground black pepper

Tomato Salsa
2 cups diced tomatoes
¼ cup chopped chives or green onions
1 tablespoon chopped cilantro
1 tablespoon fresh lime juice
2 tablespoons extra virgin olive oil
Salt and pepper

Bonnie's Tip:
Unsweetened coconut milk is usually found in the Asian section of supermarkets. If it has separated into layers, just whisk it together and it will be fine.

1. For the Beans: Heat oil in a large skillet over medium heat. Add peppers, onion and garlic. Cook 1 or 2 minutes over medium heat, stirring frequently. Add black beans, vinegar and ground red pepper. Bring the mixture to a boil. Simmer 2 to 3 minutes. Stir in cilantro. Season to taste with salt and pepper.

2. For the Tomato Salsa: Combine all tomato salsa ingredients in a small bowl.

3. To serve: Place a mound of Coconut Cilantro Rice on plate or platter; top with black beans and garnish with Tomato Salsa. Makes 6 to 8 servings

COCONUT CILANTRO RICE

You will be pleasantly surprised by the outstanding flavor created by the coconut milk.

2 tablespoons vegetable oil
2 cups long grain rice
2 cups chicken broth
1 (14-ounce) can unsweetened coconut milk
½ teaspoon ground cumin
¼ to ½ cup chopped fresh cilantro
Salt and pepper

1. Place oil in heavy saucepan over medium heat. Add rice; cook 1 minute.

2. Add chicken broth, coconut milk and cumin. Bring to a boil, cover, reduce heat and simmer for 20 minutes or until rice is cooked and liquid is absorbed. Stir in cilantro. Season to taste with salt and pepper. Makes 6 to 8 servings

KEY LIME TART IN COCONUT CRUST

Key Limes are a variety of tiny, very tart limes found in South Florida. Most markets in large urban areas carry them. I have substituted bottled Key Lime juice in this recipe with very good results.

Coconut Crust
1½ cups graham cracker crumbs
¾ cup shredded coconut
¼ cup sugar
½ teaspoon cinnamon
⅓ cup butter, melted
½ teaspoon vanilla extract

Filling
4 large egg yolks
1 cup sugar
½ cup Key Lime juice
1 (14-ounce) can sweetened condensed
   milk
1 teaspoon vanilla extract

Whipped Cream
1 cup heavy cream
¼ cup powdered sugar
1 teaspoon vanilla extract
Garnish: Toasted coconut and/or lime
   zest (optional)

1. To make the Crust: Preheat oven to 350°F. Combine graham cracker crumbs, coconut, sugar and cinnamon in a bowl. Stir in melted butter and vanilla. Press into bottom and sides of a 9-inch tart pan. Bake 10 to 12 minutes or until golden. Cool.

2. To make the Filling: Lightly whisk eggs yolks in a mixing bowl. Whisk in sugar, Key Lime juice, sweetened condensed milk and vanilla. Pour into cooled crust and bake for 20 minutes. Remove from oven and cool to room temperature. Chill pie several hours or overnight.

3. To make the Whipped Cream: Place cream in a mixing bowl and beat with electric mixer until soft peaks form. Add sugar and vanilla, and continue to beat until stiff. Spread or pipe over pie. Garnish with toasted coconut and/or slivers of lime zest.
Makes one 9-inch tart

GARDEN
Party

When the flowers start blooming and the weather turns warm, we want to be outdoors enjoying nature. It's the perfect time to invite friends and family over for a garden party or a light meal served on the patio or deck. This menu features light and fresh foods, perfect for outdoor entertaining. It would also be nice for showers, luncheons or other special events.

People who seem to entertain so naturally are good organizers and do much preparation in advance. The beauty of this menu is that much of it may be done before hand, which removes the last-minute pressure when you have guests coming. The melon slush and gelato may be frozen up to a week ahead of time; the glazed pecans may be made several days in advance. They will keep nicely—as long as you stay out of them! The chicken salad, muffins and pastry for the tart may be made 24 hours in advance. With all that done, you are free to enjoy the party.

GARDEN PARTY

Melon Slush

Smoked Salmon Cucumber Canapés

Quick Orange Glazed Pecans

Tarragon Chicken Salad

Mini Lemon Poppy Seed Muffins

Zucchini and Sun-Dried Tomato Tart

Pistachio Gelato

The beautiful silver tray above represents a special time in my life when I was a young pastor's wife, living in the parsonage of the First Christian Church of Lebanon, Missouri. One day the door bell rang and there stood Mrs. Donnelly, an elderly church member and wife of former Governor Phil Donnelly. Preparing to move to a retirement home nearby, she held this lovely silver tray in her hands and said, "Bonnie, I know you love to cook and I want you to have this silver tray that we used in the Governor's Mansion. I am not going to put it in my auction—I want you to have it." It is a cherished keepsake from a special friend and a reminder of the love and hospitality our family experienced in that community.

Years later, I used the tray as the base of my presentation of Coco Lopez Soufflé which won the Grand Prize in the Borden's Coco Lopez contest, but here it serves up the lovely Melon Slush!

MELON SLUSH

Enjoy the party with this refreshing melon drink! The most difficult part of making this recipe is to remember to freeze the watermelon the day before.

8 cups cubed fresh seedless watermelon
2 cups lemon-lime carbonated soda
6 ounces frozen pink lemonade
    concentrate
Garnish: Lemon slices or mint leaves

1. Place melon cubes in a single layer in freezer bag and freeze flat at least 8 hours. Remove from freezer 15 minutes before making the slush.

2. Place 4 cups watermelon cubes, 1 cup lemon-lime carbonated soda and 3 ounces of pink lemonade concentrate in blender. Blend until smooth. Pour into a large serving pitcher. Repeat with remaining ingredients and add to the pitcher.

3. Pour into glasses, garnish as desired and serve. Makes 6 servings

QUICK ORANGE GLAZED PECANS

Quick to make and so good, you may want to make an extra batch just for yourself! These are good keepers and may be made several days in advance and stored in a zipper-top bag.

½ cup firmly packed brown sugar
2 tablespoons orange juice
2 cups pecan halves

Mix all together and put in a glass pie plate and microwave on High 4 to 6 minutes, stirring every 2 minutes until bubbly and brown. (See margin for differences in microwaves.) Spread in a single layer on a buttered or foil-lined cookie sheet. Cool completely.

SMOKED SALMON CUCUMBER CANAPÉS

2 large English cucumbers, cut into ½ inch slices (note on p. 70 about this type of
    cucumber)
1 (5 or 6-ounce) carton of French herb cheese (prefer Allouette or Boursin)
About 3 ounces smoked salmon
Garnish: Dill sprigs (or parsley), chopped red bell pepper

1. Using a small melon baller, scoop out a small "well" in each cucumber slice, leaving the bottom part intact.

2. Spoon or pipe a bit of the cheese into the hollowed-out space; top with a small piece of smoked salmon. Garnish as desired with dill sprigs (or parsley) and chopped red bell pepper. Makes 32 to 40 canapés

Option: If desired, cucumber canapés may be placed on top of small circles of rye bread. "Glue" together with a small dab of cheese.

Bonnie's Tip:
Cooking time and setting depends on microwave wattage. If you have a high wattage microwave, use a lower setting, such as medium, and check the pecans more often. The sugar has to boil and the pecans will begin to look very dark. If making more than one batch, you have to start with a clean dish or the sugar left in the bowl will burn.

TARRAGON CHICKEN SALAD

This is one of the best chicken salads I have ever had! It always gets rave reviews. It can be made a day ahead as it holds up very well.

Dressing
½ cup mayonnaise (prefer Hellmann's)
2 tablespoons minced onion
1 garlic clove, minced
1 tablespoon lemon juice
1 tablespoon chopped fresh tarragon
½ teaspoon salt
¼ teaspoon black pepper

Salad
3 cups diced, cooked chicken breast
¾ cup finely chopped celery
⅓ cup chopped chives or thinly sliced green onions
1 cup shredded sharp white Cheddar cheese
1 ½ cups seedless green grapes, halved
¾ cup sliced almonds, toasted
Lettuce leaves
Garnish: Chopped parsley or chives (optional)

1. Mix dressing ingredients together in a small bowl.

2. Toss chicken, celery, green onions, white Cheddar, grapes and almonds together in medium bowl. Add dressing to chicken mixture; gently fold until thoroughly mixed. Cover and chill. Scoop chicken salad on lettuce leaves and serve. Garnish as desired.

Makes 6 to 8 servings

ZUCCHINI AND SUN-DRIED TOMATO TART

This beautiful tart can also serve as a vegetarian entrée. It's good served both warm and at room temperature.

1 sheet frozen puff pastry (half of 17.3-ounce package), thawed
1 3/4 cups shredded mozzarella cheese
2/3 cup grated Parmesan cheese, divided use
1/2 cup drained oil-packed sun-dried tomatoes, thinly sliced
1/3 cup basil chiffonade (see margin note)

2 green onions, thinly sliced
1 teaspoon dried oregano
1 small zucchini, cut into thin rounds
2 large eggs
1 cup half-and-half
1/4 teaspoon salt
1/8 teaspoon ground red pepper

1. Roll puff pastry on a lightly floured surface to a 13-inch square. Using a pizza wheel, trim pastry edges to form 13-inch circle. Place pastry in an 11-inch tart pan with removable bottom. Tuck in overhang to form double-thick sides. Pierce with fork to allow steam to escape. Cover; chill at least 1 hour.

2. Preheat oven to 425°F. Place a piece of foil over the pastry, then fill it with beans or pie weights. Set tart pan on a baking sheet and bake until sides are set, about 20 minutes. Carefully remove foil and beans. Return crust to the oven and bake until bottom is golden brown, puncturing crust with fork if bubbles form, about 8 minutes. Remove from oven and cool 5 minutes.

3. Reduce oven temperature to 400°F. Sprinkle mozzarella over bottom of crust. Top with one-third cup of Parmesan. Layer sun-dried tomatoes, basil, green onions, and oregano on top of cheese layer. Arrange zucchini rounds in overlapping circles to cover top of tart.

4. Whisk eggs, half-and-half, salt, and ground red pepper in medium bowl. Pour mixture into tart. Sprinkle with remaining Parmesan cheese.

5. Bake tart until custard is set and crust is golden brown, about 35 minutes. Serve warm or at room temperature. Makes 8 servings

Bonnie's Tip:
Chiffonade is a way to cut basil leaves. Stack large basil leaves on top of one another, then roll them up from the long side; and cut crosswise into thin slivers. That, in essence, is basil chiffonade.

MINI LEMON POPPY SEED MUFFINS

These tasty little gems are packed with fresh lemon flavor with the crunch of poppy seeds. They are tasty plain but can be drizzled with icing for a special touch, if desired.

¾ cup butter, room temperature
1 ⅔ cups sugar
4 large eggs, room temperature
2 teaspoons vanilla extract
1 cup sour cream
¼ cup milk
2 ½ cups all-purpose flour
2 teaspoons baking powder
½ teaspoon baking soda
½ teaspoon salt
1 tablespoon lemon zest
2 teaspoons poppy seeds
¼ cup sliced almonds
Lemon Icing (optional)

Lemon Icing
2 cups powdered sugar
3 to 4 tablespoons fresh lemon juice
1 teaspoon lemon zest
Garnish: Lemon zest, sliced almonds
   (optional)

Bonnie's Tip:
Lemon zest is the grated or finely shredded rind of a lemon. Be sure only to remove the colored rind. The white layer underneath is called pith and is very bitter. The colored part of citrus peel contains oils that add flavor.

1. Preheat oven to 350°F. Spray two 24 mini-muffin pans with vegetable spray or line muffin pans with paper baking cups.

2. In the bowl of an electric mixer fitted with the paddle attachment, cream the butter and sugar until light and fluffy. With the mixer on low speed, add the eggs one at a time, then add the vanilla, sour cream, and milk.

3. In a separate bowl, sift together the flour, baking powder, baking soda, and salt. With the mixer on low speed add the flour mixture to the batter and beat until just mixed. Stir in lemon zest and poppy seeds. Fill each cup three-fourths full; distribute sliced almonds over the top of the muffins. Bake for 15 to 20 minutes or until the muffins are lightly browned and a cake tester comes out clean. Remove from pan and cool to room temperature. If desired, drizzle with icing.

4. For the Lemon Icing: Mix together the powdered sugar with enough lemon juice to make icing of spreading consistency. Stir in zest. Ice mini-muffins with frosting and garnish with lemon zest and sliced almonds. Makes 24 mini-muffins

PISTACHIO GELATO

Oh, this is so good! Tastes just like the gelato I enjoyed in Italy!

¾ cup unsalted shelled pistachios, lightly
   toasted
¾ cup sugar, divided use
2 cups whole milk
1 teaspoon almond extract
3 large eggs

Pinch of salt
⅔ cup cream
2 tablespoons amaretto (almond liqueur)
2 or 3 drops green food coloring
¼ cup chopped toasted pistachios
Garnish: Chopped pistachios (optional)

1. Finely grind pistachios and ¼ cup sugar in food processor. Combine pistachio mixture, milk and almond extract in medium saucepan. Cook until very hot, but not boiling.

2. Whisk eggs and remaining ½ cup sugar together in a bowl. Gradually whisk milk mixture into egg mixture and add a pinch of salt. Return to saucepan. Stir over medium heat until custard thickens slightly; do not boil. Remove from heat. Strain. Add cream, amaretto and food coloring.

3. Cool in ice bath, then refrigerate until thoroughly chilled. Process in ice cream freezer according to manufacturer's instructions.

4. When ice cream is frozen, add ¼ cup chopped pistachios. Continue to process a minute or two to mix in the pistachios. Transfer to covered container and place in freezer until ready to serve. Scoop into glasses or bowls. Garnish with chopped pistachios if desired. Makes 1 quart

Bonnie's Tip:
Toasting pistachios enhances the flavor. Place pistachios on a rimmed baking sheet and place in a preheated 350°F oven for 7 to 10 minutes or until toasted. Watch carefully, because of the oil content, they will turn from lightly toasted to burnt in a matter of minutes.

Mexican TREASURES

We are not talking gold here—we are talking taste! You will treasure the flavor and aroma of authentic Mexican ingredients skillfully combined to create a wealth of dining pleasure. This menu is definitely company worthy—get out the festive placemats, invite a few friends over and share your Mexican treasures!

Although the Mexican Rice Risotto is not a true risotto, I called it that because it is a creamy rice dish that is liberally seasoned with chiles and cheese, giving it a similarity to risotto. The tenderloin, slathered with chipotles and tempered with the sweetness of the honey and Hoisin sauce, is a wonderful mix of flavors. End the spicy meal with a rich and creamy flan.

MEXICAN TREASURES

Jicama, Orange and Red Onion Salad
with Mango Dressing

Chipotle Glazed Roasted
Pork Tenderloin

Mexican Rice Risotto

Roasted Corn, Zucchini,
Peppers and Tomatoes

Pumpkin Caramel Flan

JICAMA, ORANGE AND RED ONION SALAD WITH MANGO DRESSING

A unique salad with great flavors to accompany a Mexican meal.

Mango Dressing
1 small mango, peeled, pitted and diced
½ cup grapefruit juice
⅓ cup lime juice
1 garlic clove
1 teaspoon Dijon mustard
½ to 1 small jalapeño, seeded (leave seeds in for more "fire" as needed)
½ teaspoon salt
½ teaspoon freshly ground black pepper
⅓ to ½ cup vegetable oil

Salad
12 cups washed and dried romaine lettuce, broken into bite-sized pieces
½ jicama, peeled and cut into thin strips
½ red onion, cut into thin wedges

Garnish:
4 navel oranges, peeled, white membrane removed and sectioned
Salted, roasted pumpkin seeds

Fried tortilla strips, optional

Bonnie's Tip:
I have found the heat level of jalapeños varies greatly. Sometimes they are very hot and spicy; other times they are quite mild. I always add the smaller amount because more can be added. If you like your food hot, leave in the seeds and membrane because they are the hottest parts of chili peppers.

1. For the Dressing: Combine mango, grapefruit juice, lime juice, garlic, mustard, jalapeño, salt and pepper in blender. Process until smooth. Gradually add oil in a thin stream while machine is running; process until thickened. Taste. Adjust seasonings if desired.

2. For the Salad: Combine romaine lettuce, jicama and onion in a large bowl. Add enough dressing to moisten leaves; toss.

3. To serve: Place salad on plates. Top with orange sections. Drizzle a little additional dressing over the top. Sprinkle with pumpkin seeds and add a few fried tortilla strips if desired. Makes 6 to 8 servings

MAKING BEAUTIFUL ORANGE SEGMENTS IS EASY!

To remove the peeling and pith:
*Slice off the top and the bottom, removing both peel and pith.
Now stand orange on a cutting board. With a sharp knife, start at
the top and trim off strips of the peeling and pith all the way
around the orange.*

To remove orange segments:
*With a sharp paring knife, slice down each side of the membrane of
the orange segment; remove and place in a bowl. Continue all the
way around the orange until they are all removed.*

CHIPOTLE GLAZED ROASTED PORK TENDERLOIN

This glaze is sweet, hot and spicy—a wonderful contrast with the juicy pork.

2 (about 1 ½ to 2 pounds) pork
    tenderloins
1 teaspoon salt
¼ teaspoon black pepper
2 canned chipotle chiles in adobo sauce

2 cloves garlic
3 tablespoons Hoisin sauce
3 tablespoons honey
2 teaspoons chopped fresh rosemary

1. Preheat oven to 450°F. Pat pork tenderloin dry. Trim off any silver skin that remains. Season with salt and pepper. Place on foil-lined baking sheet.

2. In the bowl of a food processor or blender, puree chipotles in adobe sauce with garlic, Hoisin and honey. Stir in rosemary. Spread chile mixture over top and sides of pork.

3. Roast in middle of oven for 30 minutes or until center registers 150°F. Allow to rest for 5 to 10 minutes before slicing and serving. Makes 6 servings

Bonnie's Tip:
Canned chipotle chiles in adobo sauce can be found in the Hispanic section of most large supermarkets. They are quite spicy.

You will seldom need the whole can, but they may be arranged on a parchment-lined sheet pan, frozen and then placed in a zipper-top freezer bag. Drop in the freezer and you will have them handy next time you need a chipotle.

ROASTED CORN, ZUCCHINI, PEPPERS AND TOMATOES

A colorful mix of vegetables that makes an excellent side dish.

1 (16-ounce) package frozen corn, thawed
1 medium zucchini, cut into thirds lengthwise, then thinly sliced horizontally
1 red bell pepper, chopped
½ medium onion, peeled and cut into thin wedges

2 or 3 Roma tomatoes, seeded and chopped
2 tablespoons butter, melted
1 garlic clove, minced
½ teaspoon sugar
½ teaspoon salt
Freshly ground black pepper

1. Preheat oven to 450°F. Combine vegetables in a large bowl. Melt butter; stir in garlic, sugar, salt and pepper. Toss with vegetables. Arrange on a shallow baking sheet.

2. Roast in preheated oven for 20 minutes or until vegetables are tender and corn appears slightly "parched". Stir occasionally during roasting. Makes 6 servings

Bonnie's Tip:
Always roast vegetables in a single layer in a very hot oven so the vegetables will actually roast and not steam.

MEXICAN RICE RISOTTO

This is not the traditional red Mexican Rice and not a true risotto either, but to my way of thinking, it may be the best of both worlds! It is a creamy rice seasoned with cumin, garlic and chiles and then finished off with Monterey Jack cheese and a generous handful of chopped cilantro.

2 tablespoons butter or oil
1 ½ cups long grain white rice
2 cloves garlic, pressed
1 small jalapeño, seeded and minced
1 ½ teaspoons ground cumin
3 ½ cups chicken broth

⅓ cup half-and-half, optional
1 ½ cups shredded Monterey Jack cheese
Salt and freshly ground black pepper to taste
½ cup chopped fresh cilantro

Bonnie's Tip:
You can omit the jalapeño and substitute pepper jack cheese. If you like your food hot and spicy, do not remove the seeds from the jalapeño. The seeds and membrane are the hottest parts of the peppers.

1. Heat butter in heavy medium saucepan over medium heat. Add rice; stir and cook 1 minute. Add garlic, jalapeño and cumin. Stir and cook a few seconds until fragrant.

2. Add broth; bring to a boil. Reduce heat to medium-low and cover. Cook until rice is tender; stirring occasionally, about 20 minutes.

3. Add cream and cheese and stir until mixture is heated through. Season to taste with salt and pepper. Stir in cilantro and serve. Makes 6 to 8 servings

PUMPKIN CARAMEL FLAN

A rich, dense, cool flan: a perfect ending to a Mexican meal.

Caramel Syrup
½ cup sugar
¼ cup water

Flan
7 large eggs
1 cup sugar
2 cups heavy cream or half-and-half
1 cup canned pumpkin
1 teaspoon vanilla extract
¼ teaspoon nutmeg
½ teaspoon cinnamon
⅛ teaspoon ground cloves
Garnish: Whipped cream and/or fresh
    mint leaves

1. To make the Caramel Syrup: Combine sugar and water in a small saucepan. Stir and bring to a boil. Cook, without stirring, until golden brown and syrupy. Caramelized sugar is very hot; handle with care! Divide syrup among eight 4 ½-ounce ramekins or custard cups. Turn ramekins to coat bottom and sides with syrup. Set aside.

Bonnie's Tip:
Handle caramel syrup carefully, as it is very hot. Caramel syrup will stick to the skin and will cause a severe burn.

2. To make the Flan: Preheat oven to 350°F. Beat eggs with sugar until frothy. Stir in cream, pumpkin, vanilla, and spices. Divide custard among the prepared cups.

3. Place cups in a baking pan and pour hot water into the pan until it is about half way up the sides of the cups. Bake flan for 30 to 40 minutes or until custard is done. Test by inserting a knife point about 1 inch in from the edge of the dish. If the knife comes out clean, the flan is cooked. Cool and refrigerate. Chill overnight.

4. Serve by inverting flans on dessert plate. Garnish as desired, possibly with mint leaves or whipped cream. Makes 8 servings

Sunday SUPPER

If Sunday supper is not your tradition, maybe you should consider it, at least occasionally. There's usually time to cook and the refrigerator is well stocked from Saturday morning marketing.

It's relaxing to spend some quality time in the kitchen honing culinary skills while making a fabulous meal to share. Gathering around a table, enjoying a good meal, telling a few stories and sharing a few laughs —yes, Sunday suppers are a grand tradition!

I fell in love with Panzanella Salad in Italy, made with garden-ripe tomatoes and fresh herbs from Chef Claudio's garden. Chef told us it was peasant food, a good way to use leftover bread when tomatoes were plentiful. Since few of us have leftover bread around, I have included instructions for making the croutons; they are laced with olive oil and garlic and will soak up the tomato juices admirably. The roasted salmon is a snap to make and the side dishes will have your guests clamoring for more Sunday suppers.

SUNDAY SUPPER

Panzanella Salad

Roasted Salmon with
Lemon Butter Sauce

New Potatoes in Dill and Chive Sauce

Sautéed Zucchini and Grape Tomatoes

Peach Melba Tart

PANZANELLA SALAD

Make this salad when fresh garden tomatoes are at their peak for best flavor.

Croutons
¼ cup olive oil
1 tablespoon minced garlic
6 cups crustless day-old bread, cut into
  ½ inch cubes
6 tablespoons finely grated Parmesan
  cheese
Salt and freshly ground black pepper

Salad
2 pounds ripe tomatoes, peeled, seeded
  and diced
2 cucumbers, peeled, split lengthwise
  and sliced ½ inch thick

1 yellow or orange bell pepper, chopped
2 cups chopped romaine lettuce
¼ cup minced onion
2 tablespoons chopped fresh basil leaves
2 tablespoon chopped fresh Italian
  parsley
1 teaspoon kosher salt
Freshly ground black pepper
3 cups Croutons
2 teaspoons minced garlic
½ cup extra virgin olive oil
2 tablespoons white wine vinegar
Garnish: ½ cup shredded Parmesan
  cheese

Bonnie's Tip:
Seeding a tomato is a technique used when juice or seeds would not be ideal in the recipe. To seed a tomato, simply cut it around the equator, and holding in the palm of your hand, squeeze the seeds out into a garbage bowl or the sink.

1. For the Croutons: Preheat oven to 375°F. Combine olive oil and minced garlic in a glass measure and heat in the microwave for 15 seconds. Do not boil; just heat to infuse garlic flavor.

2. Place bread cubes in a large bowl and drizzle the oil over them, tossing to coat the bread cubes with the oil. Sprinkle with the cheese and season with salt and pepper. Transfer the bread to a baking sheet. Bake, stirring once or twice, until the croutons are crisp and lightly colored on the outside but still soft within, about 8 or 9 minutes. Let cool. Store in an airtight container.

3. For the Salad: In a bowl, combine the tomatoes, cucumber, bell pepper, romaine, onion, basil and parsley. Season with salt and pepper. Add the croutons and toss well.

Bonnie's Tip:
In most recipes dried herbs may be substituted for fresh, and vice versa. Usually the ratio is 1 part dried herb to 3 parts fresh herbs. Fresh herbs have a higher water content and it takes more of them. Fresh herbs are usually mixed in at the end of the cooking process or right before serving as their flavors dissipate quickly.

4. Combine garlic with olive oil; drizzle oil and vinegar over salad mixture. Toss to coat. Before serving, sprinkle with Parmesan cheese.
Makes 6 to 8 servings

ROASTED SALMON WITH LEMON BUTTER SAUCE

Easy and quick! I love to roast salmon, as it practically cooks itself and cleanup is easy when the baking sheet is lined with parchment or foil.

6 (6-ounce each) salmon filets
Kosher salt
Freshly ground black pepper
¼ cup white wine

Lemon Butter Sauce
1 stick (½ cup) unsalted butter
1 large garlic clove, minced
¼ cup fresh lemon juice
1 teaspoon salt
½ teaspoon freshly ground black pepper
Garnish: Fresh dill, lemon wedge
   (optional)

1. Preheat the oven to 325°F. Season salmon with salt and pepper and place on a very lightly oiled ovenproof baking pan (or line pan with foil or parchment paper for easy clean up). Skinless salmon filets may be used. However, if the skin is still on the filets, place the skin side down on the baking sheet. Drizzle wine over the top. Roast the salmon until just cooked through, about 20 minutes.

2. For the Lemon Butter Sauce: Place butter in glass measure. Microwave for 30 to 45 seconds or until butter is just melted. Whisk in garlic and lemon juice. Season to taste with salt and pepper.

3. To serve: Drizzle with Lemon Butter Sauce and garnish with fresh dill and lemon wedge. Makes 6 servings

Bonnie's Tip:
To make fresh lemon juice, use room temperature lemons. Roll on the countertop with the palm of your hand to break down the membranes so the juice will release easily. Cut the lemon in half around the equator, and twist with a fork or lemon reamer while squeezing the juice from the lemon. Strain to remove seeds.

NEW POTATOES IN DILL AND CHIVE SAUCE

2 pounds small new potatoes, scrubbed but not peeled
½ cup sour cream
3 tablespoons chopped fresh chives

1 tablespoon chopped fresh dill (or 1 teaspoon dried dill weed)
Salt and freshly ground black pepper to taste

1. If potatoes are small, peel a thin strip from around the equator of each potato. If larger, cut in halves or quarter, but leave the peel on.

2. Place potatoes in a large saucepan, cover with salted water by 1 inch, bring to a boil then reduce heat and simmer until just tender, about 15 to 20 minutes. Drain potatoes in a colander.

3. Return potatoes to pan. Add sour cream, chives and dill. Season with freshly ground black pepper. Toss to coat potatoes. Taste and adjust salt if necessary. Serve potatoes warm. Makes 6 to 8 servings

SAUTÉED ZUCCHINI AND GRAPE TOMATOES

A quick and easy side dish that can be made in minutes.

2 tablespoons olive oil
1 garlic clove, minced
2 pounds fresh zucchini, halved
   lengthwise and sliced diagonally
1 cup grape tomatoes, halved

¼ cup freshly grated Parmesan cheese
½ teaspoon salt
½ teaspoon freshly ground pepper

1. Heat oil and garlic in heavy skillet over medium heat; cook until fragrant, but not browned.

2. Stir in zucchini, stir fry until tender-crisp. Add tomatoes, stirring until heated. Add remaining ingredients. Toss to combine; serve immediately. Makes 6 servings

'PARMESAN CHEESE'...

refers to domestic Parmesan cheese. It is readily available as a wedge, grated and shredded in supermarkets and is fine in many recipes. Be wary of brands that come in a can that contain fillers—they will not perform as well. 'Parmigiano-Reggiano' is authentic Italian cheese that is produced only in certain provinces in Italy under strict guidelines. Under Italian law, only those cheeses can be labeled Parmigiano-Reggiano.

PEACH MELBA TART

This is best when made with tree-ripened, juicy peaches. It's a beautiful and scrumptious dessert!

Crust
12 graham crackers (or 1 ½ cup graham cracker crumbs)
⅓ cup sugar
¾ cup whole almonds, lightly toasted and chopped
½ cup butter, melted

Filling
1 (14-ounce) can sweetened condensed milk
⅓ cup fresh lemon juice
1 (8-ounce) package cream cheese, softened to room temperature
1 tablespoon amaretto liqueur (or ½ teaspoon almond extract)
1 teaspoon vanilla extract
2 or 3 large, fresh peaches, peeled and sliced
(use lemon juice or Fruit Fresh, optional, to preserve color of peaches)
1 cup fresh raspberries
3 tablespoons peach preserves, warmed and strained
Garnish: Powdered sugar and fresh mint leaves (optional)

Bonnie's Tip:
You will need an 11-inch-tart pan to make this recipe. Prebaking the crust creates a crisp crust that holds together and serves nicely.

Fruit Fresh is a commercially prepared powder that keeps fruit from oxidizing and turning brown. It is basically ascorbic acid, or Vitamin C.

1. For the Crust: Preheat oven to 350°F. Process 12 broken graham crackers in food processor to make crumbs. You should have 1 ½ cups crumbs. Add sugar and almonds to food processor bowl and process until almonds are finely chopped. Add butter; pulse a few times to mix.

2. Butter or spray with cooking spray an 11-inch-tart pan. Press crumbs firmly into bottom and up sides of pan. I like to place plastic wrap over the crumbs and press firmly with fingers. Be sure to press firmly along the sides of the pan so the crust will hold together and then remove plastic wrap. Bake 10 minutes. Cool. Set aside.

3. For the Filling: Combine sweetened condensed milk in a bowl and stir in lemon juice. Set aside. Beat cream cheese until soft and creamy and mix in with condensed milk. Add amaretto and vanilla. Pour into crust; cover and chill several hours or overnight.

4. For the Topping: Peel and slice peaches. If not serving immediately, sprinkle with Fruit Fresh (or sweetened lemon juice) to preserve color. Arrange peaches and fresh raspberries over top of tart. Brush fruit with peach preserves as a glaze for a shiny finish. Garnish with powdered sugar and fresh mint if desired. Makes one 11-inch tart

LAKE FOOD, PICNICS, DINING *al* FRESCO

If you are heading to the lake for a holiday weekend or planning a picnic, or perhaps you need to "take a dish," this menu would be great. The food is easily made ahead and transports beautifully. Even if you have no such plans, the summery fare would be very nice to savor on your deck on a warm summer evening or even enjoy in the air-conditioned kitchen. The food is made in advance, is beautiful, easy to transport, and above all — tastes delicious.

For a stimulating starter, nothing beats a glass of refreshing gazpacho. Who would have ever thought vegetables could taste this good? The Muffuletta is a long-time favorite of mine. When I make it in a cooking class, my students cannot believe how gorgeous it is when cut; and then when tasted, the ratings skyrocket! The Key Lime Bars boast a thin layer of lime filling — sweet and tart at the same time. Just one amazing menu!

LAKE FOOD, PICNICS, DINING AL FRESCO

Spicy Spanish Gazpacho

New Orleans Muffuletta

Marinated Artichoke Vegetable Salad

Fresh Fruit in Vanilla Bean Sauce

Key Lime Bars

SPICY SPANISH GAZPACHO

A spicy tomato-based soup that originated in Spain and is served chilled. It is very refreshing on a warm, summer day. For the very best flavor, make this when garden-ripe tomatoes are available.

1 hothouse cucumber, halved and
  seeded, but not peeled
2 red bell peppers, cored and seeded
2 garden ripe tomatoes
1 onion
3 garlic cloves, minced
3 cups vegetable juice (prefer V-8)
¼ cup balsamic vinegar

¼ cup good olive oil
2 tablespoons fresh chopped basil
½ tablespoon kosher salt
1 teaspoon freshly ground black pepper
¼ teaspoon ground red pepper

Hothouse cucumbers are also known as English cucumbers or European cucumbers. In local markets they are usually sealed in a tight layer of cellophane. They have very tender skin and few or no seeds. Regular cucumbers can be substituted, but remove any surplus seeds.

1. Roughly chop the cucumber, bell peppers, tomatoes, and onion into 1-inch cubes.

2. Place the steel blade in a food processor and coarsely chop each vegetable separately and place in a large bowl or container.

3. Add the garlic, juice, vinegar, olive oil, basil, salt and peppers. Mix well and chill before serving. The longer the gazpacho sits, the more the flavors develop. Makes about 1 quart

NEW ORLEANS MUFFULETTA

The muffuletta, which originated in New Orleans, makes a huge sandwich and will be a crowd pleaser. The sandwich is made in advance and is a great traveler. Just keep it chilled in the cooler until lunch time.

Olive Salad
1 cup pitted, sliced green olives
1 cup pitted, sliced black olives
⅓ cup finely chopped fresh parsley
⅓ cup roasted red peppers, drained and chopped
1 garlic clove, minced
1 tablespoon olive oil
1 tablespoon lemon juice
1 teaspoon dried oregano
Freshly ground black pepper to taste

1 round Italian loaf, approximately 8 inches in diameter
2 cups shredded lettuce
5 ounces smoked turkey breast, thinly sliced
5 ounces spicy Italian hard salami, thinly sliced
5 ounces Black Forest Ham, thinly sliced
5 slices provolone cheese, thinly sliced
5 slices Cheddar cheese, thinly sliced, optional

I have made muffuletta dozens of times—it is a stunning sandwich, beautiful on the plate, and is so scrumptious you will be bombarded with requests to make it again and again. Make it a day ahead and wrap it very tightly in plastic wrap to press it all together and it will cut beautifully and hold together when served. Perhaps the most difficult part is finding the unsliced, round loaf of bread. I usually call my supermarket a few days in advance to order the bread unsliced.

1. In a mixing bowl, combine olive salad ingredients. Set aside.

2. Cut the bread horizontally and pull out some of the excess soft dough in the middle.

3. Spread half of the olive salad mixture in the hollow bottom of the bread. Add half the lettuce, then layer the turkey, salami, ham and cheeses over the olive mixture. Top with remaining lettuce. Finally heap the remaining olive salad on the other side of the loaf. Press the sides together and tightly wrap the sandwich in plastic wrap.

4. Put the loaf in the refrigerator. Let it rest for at least 30 minutes to 24 hours.
Cut into wedges. Makes 8 servings

MARINATED ARTICHOKE VEGETABLE SALAD

A lovely "do ahead" salad that actually tastes better after it sets for a few hours. Overnight is fine, just stir in tomatoes right before serving.

2 (15-ounce) cans artichoke hearts, drained and halved
1 European cucumber, sliced (see p. 70)
1 red bell pepper, cut into thin strips
½ pound baby carrots, cooked crisp-tender, drained and chilled
1 (15-ounce) can pitted black olives, drained
½ small red onion, sliced and divided into rings
1 pint carton grape or cherry tomatoes, halved

Dressing
1 cup sugar
1 cup white wine vinegar
½ cup vegetable oil
1 ½ teaspoons salt
1 teaspoon freshly ground black pepper
¼ cup chopped fresh basil and/or chives

1. **Place** all vegetables except cherry tomatoes in a large container.

2. **Whisk** together dressing ingredients and pour over vegetables. Stir to coat vegetables with dressing. Cover and chill several hours. Before serving, stir in tomatoes. Makes 12 servings

FRESH FRUIT IN VANILLA BEAN SAUCE

Enjoy this seasonal recipe when tree-ripened, juicy peaches are plentiful in the summer time. Fresh tree-ripened nectarines could be used as well.

1 cup sugar
1 cup water
2 tablespoons fresh lemon juice
1 vanilla bean
3 ripe, juicy peaches, peeled and sliced
2 cups fresh blueberries
1 cup fresh strawberries, optional
Garnish: Mint leaves

1. **Combine** sugar, water, and lemon juice in a small saucepan. Split vanilla bean and scrape out seeds and add seeds and pod to the pan. Bring to a boil. Reduce heat and simmer for 2 minutes. Strain and cool.

2. **Add** fruit and chill. If using strawberries, stir in right before serving.

3. **Serve** garnished with a fresh mint leaf if desired. Makes 8 servings

KEY LIME BARS

Key Lime Bars may be your new favorite bar cookie. With a rich layer of lime curd on top of a crisp coconut crust, they keep well when wrapped tightly and refrigerated.

Crust
2 cups all-purpose flour
1 cup chilled butter, cut into small pieces
½ cup powdered sugar
1 cup shredded, sweetened coconut
¼ teaspoon salt

Filling
1 ½ cups sugar
4 large eggs
¾ cup Key Lime juice
2 teaspoons grated lime zest
1 teaspoon baking powder
¼ cup all-purpose flour
Additional powdered sugar for
    dusting top
1 ounce white chocolate, melted

1. **Preheat** oven to 350°F. Generously butter a 13x9-inch-baking pan.

2. **Combine** flour, butter, powdered sugar, coconut, and salt in food processor and process until moist clumps form. Press onto bottom of prepared pan. Bake until edges are golden, about 20 minutes.

3. **Whisk** sugar, eggs, Key Lime juice, lime zest, baking powder and flour in large bowl until well blended. Pour over hot crust. Bake until topping is set and lightly golden, about 25 minutes. Dust with powdered sugar. Cool in pan on rack slightly. Drizzle with white chocolate. Cool completely. Cut into squares. Makes one 9x13-inch-pan (about 72 bar cookies)

Bonnie's Tip:
To melt white chocolate, chop into very small pieces. Place in a glass measure and microwave on High for 30 seconds. Stir. If needed, microwave again in 10 second intervals, stirring each time.

DINNER *from* *the* FARMER'S MARKET

When the Farmers' Market opens each spring, I rise early so I don't miss a thing. I have learned through experience that if you are not early, much of the good stuff may be gone! In the latter years of his life, my Dad continued to grow a huge, bountiful garden brimming with fresh vegetables. Not needing all he produced, he and my mother would pack baskets of sweet garden peas, sugar snaps, baby new potatoes, bushels of green beans and boxes of rosy ripe tomatoes in his truck and head to the local farmers' market to set up their produce stand. Customers would flock to his table to fill their bags with beautiful vegetables. It did not take long for his goods to sell; often my folks were back home by 9 a.m. So if you are planning a trip to a farmer's market, just remember the best things are often the first to go!

It's summertime, and the farmers' markets are brimming with beautiful home-grown goods: fresh greens, basil for pesto, fresh rosemary which is my favorite herb for meat, fresh green beans, newly dug potatoes that still taste sweet before the sugars have turned to starch, and fresh picked berries. This menu features the pick of the crop! Select the freshest and the best from your local farmer's market and you will have a dinner to remember.

DINNER FROM THE FARMER'S MARKET

Farmers' Market Salad with Garlic Goat Cheese Medallions

Basil Pesto   Pesto Garlic Bread

Marinated Rosemary Flank Steak

Roasted New Potatoes with Horseradish

Rustic Blackberry Cobbler

FARMERS' MARKET SALAD WITH GARLIC GOAT CHEESE MEDALLIONS

This salad is wonderful in the summertime, chock full of green beans, with warm crusty goat cheese medallions. This salad would also make a lovely, light summer lunch.

Garlic Goat Cheese Medallions
1 tablespoon butter
1 small garlic clove, crushed
⅓ cup panko bread crumbs
8 ounces goat cheese, sliced into eight
   pieces

Vinaigrette
2 tablespoons red wine vinegar
1 garlic clove, minced
1 teaspoon chopped fresh thyme
1 teaspoon Dijon mustard
5 tablespoons extra virgin olive oil
Salt and pepper

Salad
1 pound fresh green beans, ends and
   strings removed
8 cups baby salad greens
1 cup cherry or grape tomatoes, halved
½ cup Kalamata olives, pitted

1. For the Garlic Goat Cheese Medallions: In a skillet, melt butter over medium heat and add crushed garlic. Cook and stir 30 seconds or until slightly golden. Remove from heat. Stir in breadcrumbs. Place goat cheese slices on a baking sheet. Pat crumb mixture on top of each cheese slice. Place under broiler for a minute or two, until crumbs are toasted; remove and allow to cool for 5 minutes.

2. For the Vinaigrette: Combine vinegar, garlic, thyme, and mustard in a small bowl. Gradually whisk in olive oil. Season to taste with salt and pepper. Set aside.

3. For the Salad: Blanch green beans in boiling, salted water for 3 to 6 minutes, until crisp-tender. The blanching time will depend upon the maturity of the green beans -- very young tender beans will be done in about 3 minutes while more mature beans will take 5 to 6 minutes. Drain and refresh in cold water to set the color. Drain again and pat dry. Green beans may be blanched and chilled 24 hours in advance. Place cooled green beans in sealed container and chill.

4. To assemble: Place salad greens in a large bowl. Add enough vinaigrette to coat lightly; toss. Arrange on large platter. Add green beans to same large bowl; add remaining dressing and toss. Place beans on top of salad greens. Scatter tomatoes and olives over the salads and garnish with goat cheese medallions.
Makes 4 main dish servings or 8 dinner salads

BASIL PESTO

A little bit of pesto packs a wallop of flavor! I make this in the summer when fresh basil is plentiful in my garden or at the Farmers' Market.

1 ½ cups fresh basil leaves, washed and
    blotted dry
3 cloves garlic
¼ cup toasted pine nuts or walnuts
½ teaspoon salt
¼ teaspoon black pepper
⅔ cup grated Parmesan cheese
½ cup extra virgin olive oil plus 1
    tablespoon to "seal"

1. Combine all ingredients except olive oil in food processor fitted with metal blade. Process until basil is finely chopped.

2. With motor running, slowly pour ½ cup olive oil and process a few seconds until all of the oil is absorbed. Stop motor; scrape sides and process for another 5 seconds.

3. Transfer pesto to a glass jar with lid or plastic container with lid. Cover pesto with remaining olive oil, which serves as a seal. Cover tightly and store in refrigerator for up to 1 week. Makes 1 cup

Bonnie's Tip:
When I make lots of pesto in the summer, I freeze it in small portions to add great flavor to pasta, soups and other recipes. To freeze: Place pesto in ice cube trays and freeze. When frozen, transfer to a freezer bag or container and return to the freezer. It is easy to remove a cube or two when needed. Pesto will keep well for 9 to 12 months frozen.

PESTO GARLIC BREAD

1 cup butter, room temperature
1 to 2 tablespoons of basil pesto
½ cup grated Parmesan cheese
1 loaf Italian or French bread

1. Combine butter, pesto and parmesean cheese, mixing well.

2. Slice bread diagonally in 1-inch thick slices. Spread one side of each slice with butter mixture. Form slices back into the original loaf shape, wrap in foil and place in a preheated 350°F oven for 12-15 minutes or until bread is hot and butter is melted.

MARINATED ROSEMARY FLANK STEAK

This marinade adds flavor to the steak and helps tenderize the meat. This cut of meat is best if cooked rare or medium rare so it retains its juices. To serve, slice it thinly across the grain.

Marinade
⅓ cup soy sauce
⅓ cup vegetable oil
2 tablespoons honey
2 tablespoons red wine
5 large garlic cloves, minced
3 tablespoons chopped fresh rosemary
   (or 1 tablespoon dried rosemary)
1 tablespoon coarsely ground black pepper

1 (2 ¼-pound) flank steak

1. Whisk together marinade ingredients in a small bowl. Place flank steak flat, without folding, in a large zipper lock bag and pour marinade over meat. Express air and seal; flatten out bag and turn a time or two to coat all sides of the steak. Place on a small tray or container in the event of leakage. Refrigerate for 2 to 6 hours.

2. Heat grill to medium-high heat or preheat broiler. Remove meat from marinade; discard marinade. Pat steak dry with paper towels; removing moisture enhances browning. Grill steak to desired doneness, about 4 minutes per side for medium-rare.

3. Transfer steak to cutting board. Let stand 5 minutes for juices to stabilize. Cut across grain into thin strips. Arrange on platter and serve. Makes 6 servings

ROASTED NEW POTATOES WITH HORSERADISH

These potatoes will quickly become a favorite. Don't let the amount of horseradish deter you; it is very mild when roasted, providing just a hint of its flavor.

3 pounds small, new potatoes (red, white or golden)
⅓ cup butter, melted
¼ cup prepared horseradish
1 tablespoon grated Parmesan cheese
1 ½ teaspoons coarse kosher salt
1 teaspoon freshly ground black pepper

1. **Scrub** potatoes well; do not peel. Place in a pot and cover with cold water. Bring to a boil and parboil 9 to 12 minutes or until potatoes are just beginning to soften, but not cooked. Drain.

2. **When** cool enough to handle, cut in half or quarters for bite-sized pieces. Place in a large bowl.

3. **Combine** butter, horseradish, Parmesan cheese, salt and pepper in a small bowl and add to potatoes, tossing until potatoes are well coated.

4. **Place** potatoes in a single layer on a rimmed baking sheet. Place in preheated 450°F oven and roast for 30 to 45 minutes or until potatoes are browned and tender. Serve hot, with additional freshly ground pepper and/or salt if desired. Makes 6 to 8 servings

Bonnie's Tip:
For a stronger horseradish flavor, combine 2 tablespoons melted butter with 2 tablespoons horseradish, and toss the mixture with the roasted potatoes after they come out of the oven. Enjoy immediately!

RUSTIC BLACKBERRY COBBLER

This recipe makes a very large cobbler and will easily serve twelve people. Any leftovers will be savored the next day.

Filling
2 cups sugar
3 tablespoons cornstarch
2 eggs, slightly beaten
1 cup sour cream
8 cups fresh blackberries (or 2 [1-pound] bags frozen blackberries, thawed)

2 tablespoons butter
Egg wash: 1 egg beaten with 1 tablespoon water
1 tablespoon sugar
Pastry (recipe follows)
Accompaniment: Vanilla ice cream

1. Stir sugar and cornstarch together in a large mixing bowl. Whisk in eggs and sour cream, mixing to combine all ingredients well. Fold in blackberries. Set aside.

2. On a lightly floured board or wide sheet of plastic wrap, roll out pastry crust ⅛-inch thick into a 16-inch circle. Place in a deep 10-inch or 11-inch skillet or baking dish. Add blackberry filling. Dot with butter. Fold overhanging edges over the top of the filling.

3. Brush top crust with egg wash; sprinkle with sugar. Set pan on a pizza pan or other baking sheet to catch any overflowing drips. Bake at 425°F for 30 minutes; reduce heat to 375°F and bake an additional 45 to 50 minutes or until filling bubbles and crust is golden brown. Serve warm with ice cream. Makes 12 servings

Pastry for Cobbler
3 cups all-purpose flour
1 tablespoon sugar
1 teaspoon salt
½ teaspoon baking powder

½ cup plus 2 tablespoons (or 5 ounces) chilled unsalted butter, cut into ½-inch pieces
½ cup chilled shortening (prefer Crisco)
7 to 8 tablespoons of ice water, maybe more if needed

1. Place flour, sugar, salt and baking powder in the bowl of the food processor fitted with steel blade. Pulse the dry ingredients together a few times just to mix.

2. Add half the butter and half the shortening; pulse 5 times, then process for 5 seconds. Add remaining butter and shortening and pulse again 5 times; process for 5 seconds or until mixture has the texture of small peas. Dump mixture into a large bowl. Slowly drizzle the cold water into the flour, tossing with a fork to blend. If the crumbs will not hold together, add a little more water, a teaspoon at time, until the dough will hold together when squeezed gently in your hand.

3. Turn the dough out onto a large piece of plastic wrap. Bring all the edges together to squeeze the dough into a mound. Flatten slightly with your palm and shape into a large disc shape. Wrap in plastic wrap and refrigerate at least 30 minutes or up to 3 days.

Bonnie's Tip:
Although not necessary, I love the look of this cobbler in a cast iron skillet. It is a beautiful, homey presentation, and the cast iron bakes the bottom crust perfectly. It has a crisp and delectable texture with the blackberry filling.

A LITTLE BIT of ITALY

The inspiration for this menu comes from "The Hill" in St. Louis, Missouri, an area sometimes referred to as "Little Italy." The Hill was settled mainly by immigrants from northern Italy

and Sicily starting in the late 19th century. I have fond memories as a child visiting the area, as my uncle married an Italian woman from The Hill. They lived on Daggett Street with her extended family members nearby; her parents were from the old country and spoke only Italian.

Most of all, I remember the delicious foods my Italian aunt cooked—rich tomato sauces, pastas, the best Italian sausage I have ever had. I have visited the area in recent years and it has changed. The tenements and goats are gone and the area has been modernized—progress, I guess. However, many authentic restaurants and markets are still in the area, and it is a fun place to visit.

If a trip to Italy or The Hill in St. Louis is not in your plans, you can still create a great Italian menu. The entrée, Chicken Asiago Spedini, is an Italian specialty that consists of rolled food; sometimes it is skewered to hold it together and for serving. My version omits that, but it certainly could be skewered, if desired. The Chocolate Hazelnut Torte is reminiscent of the Whipped Cream Cake my Italian aunt often brought to the farm when she visited. Although it appears lavishly decorated, it is quite easy with a pastry bag and a large star tip. But you will have no complaints if you choose to simply spread the chocolate whipped cream over the top!

A LITTLE BIT OF ITALY

Herb Infused Fresh Mozzarella with
Capers and Genovese Salami

Chicken Asiago Spedini

Cheese Ravioli with Garden-Ripe
Tomatoes and Spinach

Sautéed Summer Squash
with Olives and Parmesan

Chocolate Hazelnut Torte

HERB INFUSED FRESH MOZZARELLA WITH CAPERS AND GENOVESE SALAMI

Fresh mozzarella - soft, creamy and mild - is important in this recipe. Be sure to use fresh herbs and a good extra-virgin olive oil.

12 ounces fresh mozzarella cheese
⅓ cup extra virgin olive oil, divided use
2 garlic cloves, minced
1 tablespoon minced fresh basil
1 tablespoon minced fresh chives
1 teaspoon minced fresh rosemary
¼ teaspoon kosher salt

¼ teaspoon ground black pepper
2 tablespoons capers
¼ teaspoon dried crushed red pepper
½ cup sliced green olives
6 slices Genovese salami
Garnish: Fresh herbs
Accompaniments: Baguette slices or crackers

1. Slice cheese in ¼-inch-thick-slices. Overlap cheese slices on medium platter.

2. Heat 2 tablespoons oil in small skillet over medium heat. Add garlic and stir just until garlic begins to become fragrant, about 30 to 60 seconds. Remove from heat; stir in herbs, salt, and pepper. Cool to room temperature. Stir in capers and remaining oil. Spoon over cheese slices. Sprinkle cheese with crushed red pepper.

3. Place green olive slices on cheese and arrange salami around cheese. Serve with baguette slices or crackers. Garnish platter with additional fresh herbs, as desired. Makes 6 servings

Extra-virgin olive oil is made from the first pressing of the olives and has more flavor. Also, it is usually more expensive. Most supermarkets and kitchen stores will carry a nice selection of olive oils.

Oils will have a longer shelf life if you store them in a cool, dark place. Most oils are stable for 6 months or longer. Some olive oils are sold in cans, which protects the oil from light.

SAUTÉED SUMMER SQUASH WITH OLIVES AND PARMESAN

Delicious, easy, and a great way to use those summer garden vegetables.

2 tablespoons olive oil
3 green onions, chopped
1 garlic clove, minced
4 small zucchini, thinly sliced on diagonal
1 summer squash, split lengthwise, and sliced on diagonal
1 tablespoon fresh minced oregano
1 tablespoon minced fresh basil
¼ cup shredded Parmesan cheese
¼ cup Kalamata olives, coarsely chopped
1 teaspoon balsamic vinegar
Salt and crushed red pepper to taste

1. Heat olive oil in wok or large skillet over medium heat. Add onion, garlic, zucchini and summer squash.

2. Stir fry for 2 to 3 minutes over high heat until tender-crisp. Do not overcook. Reduce heat to low. Stir in herbs, Parmesan cheese, olives, and balsamic vinegar. Toss to mix. Remove from heat and season to taste with salt and crushed red pepper. Makes 6 servings

Bonnie's Tip:
Stir-frying is a technique that cooks food quickly. Food is fried in a small amount of fat while being continually stirred and tossed to quickly and evenly cook all surfaces.

CHICKEN ASIAGO SPEDINI

A most delicious way to prepare chicken breast. Chicken rolls may be made 24 hours in advance, then they are ready to brown and finish in the oven.

6 (6-ounce) boneless, skinless chicken breasts
⅓ cup olive oil
⅓ cup lemon juice
2 cloves garlic, minced
1 cup dry Italian bread crumbs
1 teaspoon salt

¼ teaspoon black pepper
Fresh basil, about 10 to 15 leaves, chopped
⅔ cup shredded Asiago cheese
Vegetable oil for frying
Garnish: Chopped fresh chives, basil or parsley

1. Line a baking sheet with parchment paper or spray with vegetable oil spray. Set aside.

2. Slice chicken breasts horizontally, but not all the way through, just enough to open up like a book. Cover with plastic wrap and flatten with a rolling pin to make uniform thickness. Repeat with each breast.

Asiago Cheese is an Italian cheese much like Parmesan and Romano. They are often used interchangeably in recipes.

3. Combine olive oil, lemon juice and minced garlic. Dip each opened chicken breast into the oil mixture, then into the Italian breadcrumbs.

4. Season with salt and pepper. Distribute basil over each chicken breast. Place about 2 tablespoons shredded cheese on each breast. Roll chicken breast by folding in sides, and rolling, placing seam-side down on baking sheet. Cover and refrigerate several hours, or overnight.

5. Preheat oven to 350°F. Heat a skillet over medium heat; add oil to a depth of ½ inch. Brown chicken rolls in hot oil, then transfer to a baking sheet. Finish cooking by placing in preheated oven for 15 to 20 minutes or until done. (Time will depend on size of chicken breasts.) To serve, cut on the diagonal and garnish with fresh herbs. Makes 6 servings

CHEESE RAVIOLI WITH GARDEN-RIPE TOMATOES AND SPINACH

A pasta-vegetable side dish that is also a wonderful vegetarian entrée.

1 (16-ounce) package cheese-filled ravioli
6 Roma tomatoes
¼ cup basil chiffonade (rolled and thinly sliced leaves, see p. 51 for technique)
¼ cup drained capers
½ teaspoon black pepper

¼ teaspoon salt
2 tablespoons butter
4 cloves garlic, minced
2 cups fresh baby spinach
½ cup shredded Parmesan cheese

1. Cook ravioli according to package directions. Drain, set aside and keep warm.

2. While ravioli is cooking, make the sauce. Cut each tomato into four wedges and place in a large bowl. Add basil, capers, pepper and salt; stir to combine and set aside.

3. Place a large skillet over medium heat. Add butter. When butter is melted, add garlic and cook for 15 to 30 seconds or just until it becomes fragrant. Do not let it brown. Add tomato mixture; cook just until it is hot and begins to simmer. Remove from heat and gently stir in spinach.

4. To serve, place warm ravioli on serving platter. Spoon tomato mixture over ravioli. Sprinkle Parmesan cheese on top. Makes 6 side-dish servings

CHOCOLATE HAZELNUT TORTE

A beautiful layered dessert of rich chocolate cake, layers of chocolate glaze and billows of whipped cream. Although this torte does not have hazelnuts in it, it is flavored with Frangelico, an Italian hazelnut liqueur. If desired, toasted hazelnuts could certainly be used to garnish the top. But it is quite wonderful just as is: rich and indulgent!

Chocolate Cake
1 cup hot, strong-brewed coffee
½ cup unsweetened cocoa powder
1 ⅓ cups plus 1 tablespoon all-purpose flour
1 teaspoon baking soda
½ teaspoon baking powder
¼ teaspoon salt
½ cup butter, room temperature
1 cup plus 2 tablespoons sugar
2 eggs
1 ½ teaspoons vanilla extract
3 tablespoons Frangelico (hazelnut liqueur)

Chocolate Glaze
1 cup heavy cream
6 ounces bittersweet chocolate chips (prefer Ghirardelli)

Chocolate Whipped Cream
2 cups heavy cream
½ cup powdered sugar
½ teaspoon vanilla
½ cup Chocolate Glaze, room temperature

Generally, flour is measured by the stir and dip method. Stir the flour to lighten it and lightly spoon flour into the measuring cup. Level the top with a flat spatula. I only sift flour when making a very light cake, such as angel food cake or chiffon cakes.

Bonnie's Tip:
For a beautiful finish, place remaining chocolate whipped cream in an 18-inch-pastry bag fitted with a large star tip. Pipe large rosettes around the perimeter of the cake. Garnish with chocolate curls.

1. For the Cake: Preheat oven to 350°F. Line a 9-inch-springform pan with parchment paper. In a medium bowl, whisk together hot coffee and cocoa until smooth. Set aside and let mixture cool.

2. Sift together flour, baking soda, baking powder and salt. Set aside. With an electric mixer, beat butter and sugar together in a large bowl until light and fluffy. Beat in eggs one at a time, and then stir in vanilla.

3. Add the flour mixture alternately with the cocoa-coffee mixture, starting and ending with the flour mixture. Spread batter evenly in the prepared pan. Bake in preheated oven for 25 to 30 minutes or until cake tests done with a wooden pick. Cool on rack for 10 minutes. Then remove cake from pan and cool completely.

4. For the Chocolate Glaze: Heat cream until it just reaches a simmer; remove from heat and stir in chocolate. Continue stirring until chocolate melts. Remove ½ cup and set aside for the whipped cream.

5. For the Chocolate Whipped Cream: Whip chilled cream in a deep bowl until soft peaks form. Whip in sugar and vanilla. Stir 1 cup whipped cream into ½ cup chocolate glaze to lighten it. Then fold into the rest of the whipped cream.

6. To assemble Cake: Split cake in half horizontally. Using half the Frangelico, brush bottom layer of cake with the liqueur. Spread ½ cup chocolate glaze over the cake. Using half the chocolate whipped cream spread a thick layer over the chocolate glaze. Place top on the cake; brush top with remaining Frangelico. Spread remaining chocolate glaze over the top of the cake. Top with remaining chocolate whipped cream and garnish with chocolate curls. Refrigerate until serving time. Makes 12 servings

TASTE *of* TEXAS

Texans have a great sense of humor and enjoy the art of conversation. This menu will certainly get people talking—probably about the fabulous food! I first had real Texas brisket in Fort Worth at Walter Jetton's—the one and the same that catered barbecues for President Lyndon B. Johnson at the LBJ ranch. Now, I don't dig a pit and smoke the meat in true Walter Jetton fashion; I have streamlined my method but the flavor is still as big as Texas!

The Black Bean and Corn Salsa is as colorful as Texas, with a jalapeño kick. It's sure to get the conversation started. The brisket will take a little time, but it is not difficult and well worth the long, slow braising time. When it's done, and you slice up the tender brisket and put a few slabs on a plate along with Tall Texas Tater Towers and a big dab of Texas Slaw, then you have a meal worthy to be called a Taste of Texas!

TASTE OF TEXAS

Black Bean and Corn Salsa

Smoked and Slow-Braised Barbecued
Beef Brisket

Texas Slaw

Tall Texas Tater Towers

Lone Star Sheet Cake with Chocolate
Pecan Frosting

TEXAS SLAW

What makes this Texas slaw? It's big in flavor and colorful. That makes it "Texas" in my book!

"Slaw" or "cole slaw"? It is generally thought the term "cole slaw" arose in the 18th century as a partial translation from the Dutch term "koolsla," a shortening of "koolsalade," which means "cabbage salad." It was commonly called cold slaw in Britain until the 1860s when "cole" (meaning cabbage) was revived. "Cole" originates from the Latin *colis*, meaning "cabbage," and is the origin of the Dutch word as well. However, in the South, it is referred to simply as "slaw."

1 medium head cabbage, shredded
1 large carrot, shredded
1 medium green pepper, julienned
1 medium sweet red pepper, julienned
1 medium red onion, finely chopped

Dressing
½ cup buttermilk
½ cup mayonnaise (prefer Hellmann's)
⅓ cup sugar
2 tablespoons lime juice
1 tablespoon white vinegar
½ teaspoon ground cumin
½ teaspoon salt
½ teaspoon celery seed
Dash ground red pepper

1. In a large bowl, combine all vegetables.

2. Whisk dressing ingredients together. Pour over vegetables; toss to coat. Cover and refrigerate at least one hour before serving for flavors to blend. Stir before serving. Makes 12 servings

BLACK BEAN AND CORN SALSA

One of my all-time favorite salsa recipes and it appears on my menu frequently.

1 (15-ounce) can black beans, rinsed and drained
1 ½ cups frozen corn, thawed
2 jalapeño chilis, seeded and minced
1 Roma tomato, finely chopped
2 tablespoons chopped green onion
2 tablespoons minced red bell pepper
2 tablespoons minced cilantro
2 tablespoons olive oil
1 tablespoon lime juice
½ teaspoon ground cumin
Salt and pepper

Combine all ingredients in a large container. Season to taste with salt and pepper. Cover and chill for 1 to 24 hours. Serve with tortilla chips. Makes about 3 ½ cups

SMOKED AND SLOW-BRAISED OVEN BARBECUED BEEF BRISKET

This recipe uses a stovetop smoker, which gives beautiful results. I usually use Mesquite wood chips to flavor the brisket in true Texas style, but hickory is also delicious.

1 6-pound brisket with thin layer of fat still attached

Brisket Rub Seasoning Mix
3 tablespoons paprika
2 tablespoons black pepper, coarsely ground
3 tablespoons chili powder
2 tablespoons salt
2 tablespoons dried minced onions (or 1 tablespoon onion powder)
1 tablespoon garlic powder
1 teaspoon ground cumin
½ teaspoon ground red pepper (or more or less to taste)

¼ cup Worcestershire sauce
Barbecue Sauce, commercial or homemade

1. Trim only the heavy, thick chunks of fat from the brisket, leaving a nice layer over the meat. Combine rub seasoning mix in a small dish and rub over all surfaces of the brisket. Place meat in a large shallow pan and pour Worcestershire sauce over the meat. Cover and refrigerate for 8 to 24 hours. (May be cooked right away, but the flavors will not be as intense.)

2. Line the pan of the smoker with foil for easy clean up. Place wood chips in the bottom of the smoker and then the foil lined drip pan and then the rack. Place brisket on the rack. Pour any pan juices over the top of the meat. Place lid on smoker. Smoke over medium heat for 2 hours.

3. Carefully remove lid from smoker. Sometimes the heat will expand the pan and the lid may be difficult to move. Just grab a pair of pliers to assist the cook with the task: it works every time!

4. Cover surface of meat with barbecue sauce. Either replace the lid or cover the pan tightly with foil and place in 300°F oven and cook very slowly for 2 to 3 hours or until the meat is very tender. (Cooking time will depend partly upon the size of the brisket.)

5. Let rest for 15 to 20 minutes, and slice across the grain and serve with additional warmed barbecue sauce if desired. Makes 10 servings

Bonnie's Tip:
A stovetop smoker can be used on a gas range, electric range with coil or the grill. It is an easy and efficient way to infuse that deep, slow-smoked flavor into meat, poultry and fish. Stovetop smokers can be purchased at specialty cookware stores.

TALL TEXAS TATER TOWERS

This is an astonishing presentation of potatoes. Instead of lying flat on the plate, they are "standing tall." Select uniform shaped ones for best presentation.

8 large russet potatoes (10 to 12 ounces each)
¼ cup butter
½ to ⅔ cup half-and-half
½ cup sour cream
½ to 1 teaspoon salt
¼ teaspoon black pepper

1 cup shredded sharp white Cheddar cheese
½ cup thinly sliced green onions
½ cup cooked and crumbled bacon
Garnishes:
1 cup shredded Cheddar cheese
¼ cup crumbled cooked bacon
Chopped chives or scallions

1. Heat oven to 425°F. Scrub potatoes and pierce tops with fork several times. Bake potatoes on oven rack 60 to 70 minutes or until tender when pierced. Remove from oven and cool 10 to 15 minutes or until cool enough to handle. Cut a thin slice off one end of the potato so it will stand up on its end.

2. Cut a thin slice off the other end of each potato. Using a teaspoon, scoop out center of each, leaving the shell intact; place shell aside. Place potato pulp in mixing bowl. Using electric mixer or potato masher, break up potatoes. Add butter, half-and-half, sour cream and salt and pepper. Beat until blended. Stir in cheese, green onions and bacon. Taste and adjust seasonings if desired. Spoon or pipe mixture into potato shells. Place them in muffin tins to hold them upright. Garnish the tops with remaining cheese, bacon and chives.

3. Cover and refrigerate. To serve, heat in a 325°F oven for 20 to 30 minutes or until hot. Makes 8 servings

Bonnie's Tip:
Placing stuffed potatoes in muffin tins is a great way to keep them upright and to assure they will hold their shape.

Lone Star Sheet Cake with Chocolate Pecan Frosting, p. 95

LONE STAR SHEET CAKE WITH CHOCOLATE PECAN FROSTING

This makes a rich dense cake and has been a family favorite for decades! I have made this cake dozens of times and it always disappears in a hurry. I first sampled it many years ago when I lived in Fort Worth. It has appeared in many variations over the years, but I always associate it with the Lone Star State. This cake has it all—fabulous flavor and moist texture. My version has cinnamon added, which is a dynamite combination with the chocolate. Also, it is easily made and no mixer required!

2 cups flour
2 cups sugar
½ teaspoon salt
1 cup butter
1 cup water
⅓ cup cocoa
1 teaspoon baking soda
½ cup buttermilk
2 eggs, slightly beaten
1 teaspoon vanilla extract
1 teaspoon cinnamon
Chocolate Pecan Frosting (recipe follows)
1 cup pecans, toasted and coarsely chopped

1. Preheat oven to 350°F. Grease and flour a 10 x 15-inch-jellyroll pan. Set aside.

2. Place flour, sugar and salt into a large bowl. Combine butter, water and cocoa in a small saucepan. Bring to a boil and pour over flour and sugar mixture, stirring to mix. Combine baking soda and buttermilk; then add buttermilk mixture to flour and sugar mixture, stirring to combine.

3. Add eggs, vanilla and cinnamon, stirring until ingredients are combined.

4. Pour into prepared pan and bake for 20 minutes, or until cake tests done. While cake is baking, prepare the frosting.

5. Allow cake to cool 5 to 10 minutes to firm up a bit; then pour the frosting over the warm cake. Sprinkle nuts on top. Let cool and cut in squares and serve. Makes one 10 x 15 cake

Chocolate Pecan Frosting
½ cup butter
⅓ cup cocoa
⅓ cup milk
1 (1-pound) box powdered sugar
1 teaspoon vanilla extract

Combine butter, cocoa and milk in a small saucepan over medium heat. Bring just to a simmer; do not allow to boil. Pour powdered sugar into a mixing bowl. Pour hot cocoa mixture over powdered sugar. Beat well with whisk or electric mixer until creamy. Stir in vanilla. Pour over warm cake.

Bonnie's Tip:
Buttermilk does add a delicious flavor to baked goods. However, a good substitute is to add 1 teaspoon of lemon juice or vinegar to 1 cup of milk. Also, dried buttermilk is available at supermarkets and will keep in the pantry for several months.

SOUTHWEST
Pleasures

The Southwest is mostly a dry, arid area, but its spicy cuisine can make your mouth water. Southwest food is a reflection of its Mexican, Spanish and Native American roots and this menu captures the core of the popular cooking style of the American Southwest.

The sun is not the only thing heating up the Southwest, its cuisine can, too! People have decidedly different tolerance to chile pepper and I tend to use a light hand, knowing more can always be added. The hottest part of the chile pepper is the membrane holding the seeds; if you like lots of heat, don't remove the seeds and membrane but chop them finely and add to the dish.

SOUTHWEST PLEASURES

Avocado, Tomato
and Corn Salad

Sausage Quesadillas
with Black Bean Salsa

Shredded Beef Enchiladas
with Salsa Verde

Cilantro Rice

Frozen Texas Tumbleweeds

Bonnie's Chocolate Sauce

AVOCADO, TOMATO AND CORN SALAD

Easy to toss together for summer dining. Nice with all grilled foods. If making ahead, leave out the avocado and mix it in right before serving.

2 ½ cups frozen corn, thawed
2 avocados, cut into ½ inch cubes
2 ½ cups grape tomatoes, halved
8 ounces sharp white Cheddar cheese, shredded or cut in very small cubes
½ cup finely diced red onion

Dressing
3 tablespoons olive oil
3 tablespoons fresh lime juice
1 teaspoon grated lime zest
⅓ cup chopped cilantro
½ teaspoon salt
¼ teaspoon pepper

1. Combine the corn, avocado, tomatoes, Cheddar cheese and onion in a large glass bowl.

2. Mix together the dressing ingredients in another bowl, pour over the salad and gently toss to mix. Makes 8 servings

SAUSAGE QUESADILLAS WITH BLACK BEAN SALSA

I took the Grand Prize in a national contest for food professionals sponsored by the National Livestock and Meat Board with this recipe. The quesadilla makes a great starter for a party but also would make a tasty brunch or lunch. Although the recipe is in two parts, it is amazingly easy to do.

1 pound hot, bulk pork sausage
8 (7-inch) flour tortillas
1 ½ cups (6 ounces) shredded Cheddar cheese
1 ½ cups (6 ounces) shredded Monterey Jack cheese
1 jalapeño pepper, seeded and finely chopped (optional)
1 tablespoon vegetable oil or melted butter
Garnishes: Sour cream and cilantro (optional)
Black Bean Salsa (recipe follows)

1. Cook sausage in skillet over medium heat until browned. Drain; set aside.

2. Spread four tortillas on cookie sheet. Divide sausage and cheeses evenly over the four tortillas. Sprinkle on jalapeño peppers if desired. Place remaining tortillas over sausage mixture, pressing down firmly. Brush tops with oil. Bake at 400°F for 7 to 10 minutes, or until lightly browned.

3. To serve, place each quesadilla on a plate. Cut quesadillas into six wedges. Garnish as desired. Push wedges apart to make a space in the middle. Place a scoop of Black Bean Salsa in center of each one.

Black Bean Salsa
1 (16-ounce) can black beans, rinsed and drained
¾ cup frozen corn kernels, thawed
1 medium tomato, seeded and diced
2 tablespoons minced cilantro
5 green onions, thinly sliced (green tops included)
3 tablespoons extra virgin olive oil
1 tablespoon red wine vinegar
1 clove garlic, crushed
½ teaspoon ground cumin
Salt and freshly ground black pepper

Combine beans, corn, tomato, cilantro and onions in a bowl. Whisk together olive oil, vinegar, garlic, cumin and salt and pepper to taste. Pour over vegetables. Toss to coat. Cover and chill. Makes 8 appetizers or 4 main-dish servings

SHREDDED BEEF ENCHILADAS WITH SALSA VERDE

This recipe takes awhile to make but is so worth the effort. Look at it as two different recipes: one for the meat and one for the sauce. Then you simply put them together - and it's done!

2 ½ pound boneless beef chuck roast, cut into 8 pieces
1 tablespoon vegetable oil
1 small onion, chopped
2 jalapeño peppers, seeded and finely chopped
2 cloves garlic, minced
½ cup beef broth
1 ½ teaspoons chili powder
½ teaspoon ground cumin
½ teaspoon salt
⅛ teaspoon ground red pepper
8 corn or flour tortillas (6 to 7 inch)

Salsa Verde
3 poblano chiles
3 Anaheim chiles
½ cup vegetable oil
1 medium onion, chopped
1 cup chopped green onion
2 cloves garlic, minced
1 to 2 teaspoons salt
1 ½ teaspoon dried basil
1 ½ teaspoon ground cumin
1 ½ teaspoon dried leaf oregano
1 teaspoon black pepper
⅔ cup flour
4 cups chicken broth
2 tablespoons lime juice
1 cup (4 ounces) shredded Cheddar cheese

Optional Garnishes: Sour cream, sliced green onions, chopped cilantro, chopped tomatoes, and black olives

1. Heat oil in Dutch oven over medium high heat until hot. Cook onion, jalapeño peppers and garlic in hot oil 2 minutes, stirring frequently. Add beef chuck pieces and broth; sprinkle with chili powder, cumin, ground red pepper and salt. Cover with a tight-fitting lid and place in a preheated 325°F oven and cook for 2 ½ hours or until very tender. (I often put it all in the crockpot early in the day, turn it on low and it is perfect 8 hours later.)

2. Meanwhile, make the Salsa Verde. To roast chiles, split chiles and place skin side up on a foil-lined baking sheet. Char chilies under broiler until skin is blackened. Remove from oven and carefully cover with foil and allow to steam until cool enough to handle. Peel chiles and remove seeds and chop. Set aside.

3. Heat oil in a heavy saucepan. Add onions and garlic; sauté until softened. Add 1 teaspoon salt, basil, cumin, oregano and black pepper; cook a few seconds. Add flour and cook for a minute or two. Add chicken broth, lime juice and chopped chiles; bring to a boil, stirring constantly. Reduce heat and simmer for 5 minutes.

4. When beef is cool enough to handle, shred, removing all fat and connective tissue. Mix shredded beef well with pan juices.

5. Preheat oven to 375°F. Spread small amount of salsa in bottom of 9 x 13-inch-baking dish. You want just enough to cover the bottom with a thin layer.

6. Wrap tortillas in a damp paper towel and warm in microwave 60 seconds or until warm. Divide meat mixture evenly among tortillas. Roll each up tightly. Place tortillas, seam side down, in prepared baking dish. Spread remaining salsa verde evenly over top of enchiladas. Sprinkle evenly with cheese.

7. Bake for 15 to 20 minutes or until hot. Garnish as desired. Makes 8 servings

Bonnie's Tip:
Meat may be cooked a day in advance. Cool slightly, then cover and refrigerate in its own juices until ready to use.

The enchiladas can be made, assembled and refrigerated 24 hours in advance. It will take 10 to 15 minutes longer in the oven, so plan accordingly.

CILANTRO RICE

A tasty, well-seasoned rice that is a perfect partner to Southwestern food.

2 tablespoons olive oil
1 red bell pepper, seeded and diced
1 small onion, peeled and chopped
1 jalapeño, minced
1 clove garlic, minced
1 cup long grain, uncooked rice
1 ½ cups chicken stock
½ cup chunky salsa
¾ teaspoon ground cumin
½ cup chopped fresh cilantro
½ cup sliced black olives
Salt and pepper to taste

1. **Place** oil in heavy saucepan over medium heat. Add bell pepper, onion, jalapeño and garlic. Sauté for 2 to 3 minutes or until vegetables are fragrant. Stir in rice; cook 1 minute.

2. **Add** chicken broth, salsa and cumin. Cover and simmer for 20 minutes or until rice is cooked and liquid is absorbed. Stir in cilantro and black olives. Serve immediately.

Makes 4 servings

FROZEN TEXAS TUMBLEWEEDS

Though traditionally served as a drink, I freeze this mixture and serve it as a frozen dessert. A perfect ending!

½ gallon good-quality vanilla ice cream (such as Blue Bell or Breyer's All-Natural Vanilla)
⅓ cup coffee liqueur
¼ cup clear crème de cacao liqueur
Chocolate Sauce (recipe follows or use purchased sauce)
Garnish: Toasted pecans, coarsely chopped

1. Set out ice cream 10 minutes to soften slightly. It should be soft but not melted.

2. In a large bowl, combine ice cream, coffee liqueur and crème de cacao. Mix just until blended; work quickly so ice cream does not melt.

3. Pour into container and freeze for several hours or overnight. Scoop into pretty dessert dishes or glasses; spoon chocolate sauce over the top. Garnish with toasted pecans.
Makes 8 to 12 servings

Bonnie's Tip:
Refrigerated sauce becomes very thick. Remove the lid and rewarm gently over low heat or on low power in microwave.

BONNIE'S CHOCOLATE SAUCE

So delicious you may want to keep this on hand in your refrigerator.

1 cup heavy cream
½ cup sugar
2 tablespoons light corn syrup
2 tablespoons butter
8 ounces bittersweet or semi-sweet chocolate chips
1 teaspoon vanilla

Combine cream, sugar, syrup, and butter in a small heavy saucepan. Stir over medium heat until it comes to a boil. Add chocolate and stir over low heat until thick and smooth. Stir in vanilla. Serve sauce warm over ice cream.

TEXAS TRIES TO CLAIM IT, BUT...

The Tumbleweed drink was surprisingly first created in Wichita by bartender Everett Bonner in 1958. The drink quickly gained national popularity. Everett, at age 82 was still tending bar at the Crown Uptown Dinner Theatre, where he is a legend. Thanks, Everett for the inspiration for my version which is easy to serve to a group and make ahead of time and great served with the chocolate sauce.

Steak *HOUSE* DINNER

Steakhouse dinners have no boundaries, no limits and no zip codes. Steakhouses draw us like a magnet when we crave a tender, thick, juicy steak. No longer will you need to shell out a small mint at the local steakhouse in order to enjoy a terrific steak dinner. Fire up the grill, recreate this menu and your steak dinner will rival the best steakhouse in the state.

Nothing can beat a seared, tender and juicy steak, still sizzling from the grill. This Steak House Dinner provides it all--a beautiful, marinated steak, complete with classic side dishes and topped off with a decadent dessert of Chocolate Molten Lava Cakes with two sauces. Awesome, easy and impressive!

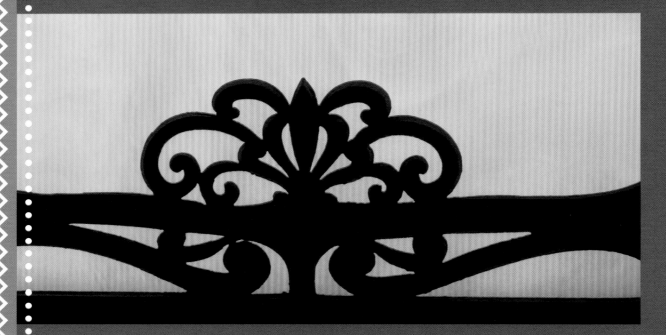

STEAK HOUSE DINNER

Caesar Salad with Lemony Garlic Dressing

Bourbon and Brown Sugar
Marinated Strip Steaks

Roasted Potatoes with Herbs

Creamy Garlic Spinach

Chocolate Molten Lava Cakes
with Two Sauces

CAESAR SALAD WITH LEMONY GARLIC DRESSING

This is a really good Caesar without the use of raw eggs. Instead, I use a bit of sour cream to create a creamy emulsion.

Dressing
2 tablespoons white wine vinegar
2 tablespoons fresh lemon juice
1 tablespoon Worcestershire sauce
1 teaspoon Dijon mustard
1 teaspoon anchovy paste
2 cloves garlic, minced
3 drops Tabasco sauce
½ teaspoon salt
½ cup extra virgin olive oil
1 tablespoon sour cream

Salad
1 large head Romaine lettuce, washed and torn into bite-size pieces (about 10 to 12 cups)
1 cup croutons
⅓ cup shredded Parmesan cheese
Freshly ground black pepper

1. Whisk vinegar, lemon juice, Worcestershire sauce, mustard, anchovy paste, garlic, Tabasco and salt in a small, deep bowl.

2. Slowly whisk in olive oil to make an emulsion. Stir in sour cream.

3. Place lettuce in a large bowl. Add salad dressing and toss to coat. Stir in croutons, Parmesan cheese and fresh ground pepper to taste.
Makes 6 servings

ROASTED POTATOES WITH HERBS

These are so good. By parboiling them first to slightly cook them, they roast quicker but the interior stays moist and creamy while the outside is roasted and caramelized.

3 pounds Yukon Gold or red-skin potatoes
½ medium onion, chopped
½ cup olive oil
3 tablespoons grated Parmesan cheese
1 tablespoon coarse kosher salt
1 teaspoon ground black pepper
⅓ cup chopped fresh parsley, divided
1 tablespoon chopped fresh rosemary
Garnish: Additional parsley or rosemary

1. **Scrub** potatoes well. Do not peel but cut each into quarters and then into bite-sized pieces. Add potatoes to large pot of boiling salted water. Cook 8 minutes and drain.

2. **Preheat** oven to 400°F. Line two rimmed baking sheets with foil or parchment paper for easy cleanup. Divide potatoes between prepared baking sheets. Toss potatoes with onions, Parmesan cheese, oil, salt, and pepper. Roast 35 minutes.

3. **Sprinkle** half of parsley and half of rosemary over potatoes on each sheet. Using metal spatula, turn potatoes to coat. Roast until brown and tender, about 20 minutes longer. Transfer to serving bowl, garnish with additional parsley or rosemary. Makes 6 to 8 servings

CREAMY GARLIC SPINACH

Creamed spinach is a steakhouse specialty. This version uses a small amount of nutmeg which is a classic seasoning for dark greens. It is not overpowering but just enough to enhance the spinach.

1 cup water
24 ounces bagged baby spinach leaves
¼ cup butter
⅓ cup chopped onion
2 garlic cloves, minced
¼ cup all-purpose flour
¼ teaspoon salt
1 ¼ cups whole milk
½ cup heavy cream
¼ teaspoon ground nutmeg
¼ teaspoon black pepper

Bonnie's Tip:
Be sure to remove as much water as you can from the cooked spinach; otherwise, the finished dish may be watery, rather than creamy.

1. **Bring** water to boil in large pot. Add half of spinach to pot; toss until wilted but still bright green, about 3 minutes. Add remaining spinach and toss until just wilted.

2. **Transfer** spinach to strainer set over large bowl. Press on spinach to release all liquid. Transfer spinach to work surface; coarsely chop. Cover and refrigerate. (Can be prepared 1 day ahead.)

3. **Melt** butter in heavy medium saucepan over medium heat. Add onion and garlic; sauté until onion is soft but not brown, about 3 minutes. Whisk in flour and salt. Cook until mixture is pale gold, whisking constantly, about 3 minutes.

4. **Whisk** in milk and cream. Boil until thick, stirring constantly, about 2 minutes. Season with nutmeg and pepper. Add spinach and stir until heated through. Taste and adjust seasonings if desired. Makes 6 servings

MOST GRILLING EXPERTS *use the hand test to tell the temperature of the fire. If you can hold your hand 5 inches above the hot grates for no more than two seconds, you have a hot fire. If you can hold your hand there for four seconds, the fire is medium-hot; and if you can hold your hand there for six seconds, you have a medium fire.*

BOURBON AND BROWN SUGAR MARINATED STRIP STEAKS

The bourbon-brown sugar marinade adds a depth of flavor to the steaks.

½ cup bourbon
½ cup soy sauce
½ cup brown sugar, firmly packed
¼ cup lemon juice
2 garlic cloves, minced
4 (10-ounce) New York strip steaks

1. Mix bourbon, soy sauce, brown sugar, lemon juice and garlic in a small bowl. Stir until sugar is dissolved. Place steaks in a shallow dish large enough for them to be in a single layer. Pour marinade over steaks. Cover and refrigerate for 4 to 8 hours.

2. Before grilling, set steaks out and allow to come to room temperature before grilling them so the inside will cook to the level you want without charring outside. Heat grill to medium-high heat. Grill steaks for 4 to 5 minutes a side for medium rare or longer if desired. Allow steak to rest for a few minutes before serving to allow juices to stabilize.

Bonnie's Tip:
Kansas City strips, New York strip, shell steak, Delmonico or just strip steak are all names for the same cut of meat. Don't let the various names confuse you. I tend to prefer Kansas City strip because I am from Kansas, known for producing great beef.

CHOCOLATE MOLTEN LAVA CAKES WITH TWO SAUCES

The ultimate dessert! My version is dusted with powdered sugar, dressed up with two sauces--Vanilla Custard Sauce and Raspberry Coulis - and served with fresh berries and a dollop of ice cream.

6 ounces bittersweet or semisweet chocolate, chopped
3 tablespoons butter
Pinch of salt
2 egg whites
4 egg yolks

¼ cup sugar, divided use
Garnish: Powdered sugar, ice cream and fresh raspberries
Vanilla Custard Sauce, recipe follows
Raspberry Coulis, recipe follows

1. **To** make the cake: Preheat oven to 425°F. Generously butter and flour four 6-ounce ramekins or custard cups.

2. **Combine** chocolate, butter and salt in a glass measure. Microwave 1 minute on high; stir; then microwave an additional 30 to 60 seconds until chocolate is melted, stirring every 15 seconds. Set aside.

3. **Using** electric mixer, beat egg whites until frothy. Continue beating and sprinkle 2 tablespoons sugar over whites, beating until soft peaks form. Set aside.

4. **In** another bowl, beat egg yolks and remaining 2 tablespoons sugar until thick and light. Fold in chocolate mixture. Gently fold whites into chocolate mixture. Divide mixture among prepared custard cups.

5. **Place** custard cups on baking sheet. Bake in preheated oven until cakes are puffed but still soft in center, about 11 minutes. Cool 2 minutes.

6. **To serve:** Using a small knife loosen cakes from edges of cups. Place serving plate on top of custard cup and invert cakes onto plates; remove cups. Drizzle Vanilla Custard Sauce and Raspberry Coulis in a decorative pattern around lava cakes. Dust with powdered sugar and serve with scoop of ice cream. Garnish with berries and serve. Makes 4 servings

RASPBERRY COULIS

Bonnie's Tip:
This makes a beautiful, uncooked crimson sauce. I find frozen berries give a deeper color than fresh ones and are always readily available in the frozen food case.

1 (12-ounce) bag frozen, unsweetened raspberries, thawed
1 teaspoon lemon juice
⅓ cup sugar

Place thawed raspberries, lemon juice and sugar in food processor. Process to blend. Run through a strainer to remove seeds. Store coulis in a covered container in the refrigerator. It will keep 7 to 10 days.

VANILLA CUSTARD SAUCE

A lovely, rich smooth sauce served cold. Make ahead; it will keep up to 5 days covered and refrigerated. May be flavored with various liqueurs for variety and to enhance various desserts.

4 egg yolks
Pinch salt
3 tablespoons sugar

1 cup half-and-half
1 teaspoon vanilla

1. Stir yolks, salt and sugar together in a small, heavy saucepan until blended.

2. Microwave half-and-half in a glass measure for 1 minute on High until scalded (or heat in a small pan until it comes to a simmer). Stir a few tablespoons into the yolks, then gradually add the rest.

3. Cook the mixture, stirring constantly, on medium heat just before the boiling point, about 170°F. Mixture will thicken and will coat the back of a wooden spoon. When a finger is run across the back of wooden spoon, it will leave a path. Immediately remove from heat. Strain into a small bowl. Stir in vanilla and cool in an ice water bath or in the refrigerator. Makes 1 ¼ cups

Bonnie's FRENCH ADVENTURE

I fondly think of my French adventure with humility and gratitude. It almost seems like a fairy tale—or at least a story too good to be true. But it happened in 2009 in Wichita, Kansas.

One of my cooking students, Hetty Bailey, who is active in the Wichita Area Sister Cities program, stayed a few moments after class one day to inquire whether I might be interested in teaching at a cooking school in France. I expressed excitement but must admit I soon dismissed the thought; it was just a bit too grand to imagine! However, a few weeks later, Hetty and her cohorts had it all arranged. I would teach at Atelier Cuisine de Laurence and be a guest in Laurence Hervé's home for five days. What an experience! Laurence was a gracious host as we explored the French markets and cooked together in her kitchen.

I had so many wonderful foods there and the markets were fabulous. The cheeses were remarkable: one market had 39 varieties of goat cheeses! I fell in love with the pastry shops filled with small pastries that were like gems, bright with fruit and colorful confections. I tried to sample most of them but am sure I missed a few; perhaps that's a good reason to return.

My French adventure coincided with "Julie and Julia" getting rave reviews in movie theaters. Julia Child had a tremendous influence on American cooking, and I was fortunate enough to have taken some master classes from her through my affiliation with the International Association of Culinary Professionals, an organization that Julia helped organize. This menu is a blend of what I learned in France and Julia's influence. The recipes are my own interpretation, but the ideas and the characteristic tastes are typically French, retaining the flavors and presentations we love.

BONNIE'S FRENCH ADVENTURE

Goat Cheese "Bricks"
with Classic Vinaigrette Salad

Beef Bourguignon

Garlic Mashed Potatoes

Individual Apple Tarts

GOAT CHEESE "BRICKS" WITH CLASSIC VINAIGRETTE SALAD

When I first saw a goat cheese "brick" on our salad plates in France, I was intrigued. They were unlike any bricks I had ever seen. They consisted of a transparent, thin sheet of pastry, usually filled and fried. I have found nothing like French bricks here in the states, but am substituting phyllo, which makes a very interesting and similar presentation.

18 sheets phyllo sheets (12 x 9 inches)
½ cup melted butter or butter-flavored cooking spray
6 ounces goat cheese, cut into six equal slices
6 thin slices bacon, cooked but still limp

Salad
8 cups leaf lettuce, washed and crisped
½ cup grape tomatoes, halved

Classic Vinaigrette Dressing
¼ cup red wine vinegar
1 teaspoon Dijon mustard
1 garlic clove, minced
1 cup extra virgin olive oil
½ teaspoon salt
¼ teaspoon black pepper

I enjoyed many salads in France, and most of them were effortlessly made with fresh greens and a simple vinaigrette. This particular one was adorned with the goat cheese brick and made a striking presentation.

1. To make the "Bricks": Preheat oven to 350°F. For each serving, remove three sheets of phyllo and place on a flat surface, keeping the rest covered with a sheet of plastic wrap so they will not dry out. Brush the top of the first sheet with melted butter (or spray with the butter-flavored spray); top with the second sheet, placing it at an angle so the corners will not line up. Brush it with butter (or spray with the butter-flavored spray) and place the third sheet on top, again at an angle so there will be several points which will make the top very festive. Brush it with butter (or spray with the butter-flavored spray).

2. Place one slice of goat cheese in the center. Bring up sides of phyllo dough to form a pouch, pressing it together right above the goat cheese. Keep the top part fluffy. Secure above the goat cheese with a strip of bacon, using a toothpick to hold it in place if necessary. Brush with butter (or spray lightly with the butter-flavored spray) and place on baking sheet. Repeat with remaining cheese and phyllo sheets. Bake until golden, about 7 to 10 minutes.

3. Meanwhile, combine greens and tomatoes in a bowl. Set aside.

4. For the Dressing: Combine vinegar, mustard and garlic in a small, deep bowl. Slowly whisk in the olive oil. Season with salt and pepper.

5. To serve: Add enough salad dressing to the greens to moisten and divide salad among six plates. Place warm goat cheese "brick" on each salad plate and serve. Makes 6 servings

BEEF BOURGUIGNON

I learned how to make Beef Bourguignon from Julia Child's book and it was delicious. However, my version is a little more straightforward and very tasty as well. I like to serve this with mashed potatoes and, of course, crusty French bread.

2 tablespoons vegetable oil
2 ½ pounds chuck beef cut into 1 inch cubes
Kosher salt
Freshly ground black pepper
1 pound carrots, peeled and sliced diagonally
  into 1 inch chunks
2 yellow onions cut into wedges
2 cloves garlic, minced
2 ½ cups burgundy or other dry red wine
2 ½ cups beef broth
2 tablespoons tomato paste
1 teaspoon dried thyme leaves
1 pound frozen pearl onions
¼ cup butter, room temperature, divided
3 tablespoons all-purpose flour
1 pound fresh mushrooms, cleaned and sliced
Garnish: ½ cup chopped fresh parsley

1. **Preheat** the oven to 325°F. Heat the oil in a large Dutch oven.

2. **Using** a paper towel, pat beef cubes dry then season with salt and pepper. Sear the beef in batches in the hot oil for 3 to 5 minutes, turning to brown on all sides. Remove the seared cubes to a plate and continue to sear remaining beef. Set aside.

3. **Add** carrots and onions to the pan; season with 1 teaspoon of salt and 1 teaspoon of pepper. Cook, stirring occasionally, until the onions are browned, about 10 minutes. Add garlic and stir for a few seconds until fragrant. Return beef to the pan.

4. **Add** the wine and beef broth; it should almost cover the meat. Add tomato paste and thyme. Bring to a simmer over medium heat.

5. **Cover** pot and place in oven for 2 hours or until the meat is very tender.

6. **Transfer** the stew to the stove top. Add the pearl onions and return stew to a boil; then reduce heat so it will simmer.

7. **Combine** 2 tablespoons butter with the flour; stir that into the stew; return to a simmer and let it thicken with the lid off, stirring now and then.

8. **Meanwhile,** brown mushrooms in the remaining 2 tablespoons of butter until lightly browned; and stir mushrooms into the stew. Simmer for 10 minutes. Taste and adjust seasonings. Serve with Garlic Mashed Potatoes with a sprinkling of fresh parsley and pass the crusty French bread. Makes 8 servings

GARLIC MASHED POTATOES

Mashed potatoes were a staple on our farm growing up and they appeared on our table regularly. One of the hardest things I had to do when I began teaching cooking classes was to write a recipe for mashed potatoes and pan gravy. Those were just two things I learned to do by sight. Mashed potatoes have been reinvented over the last 20 years with all sorts of additions to them; some good and some not so good, in my opinion. These are potatoes in their simplicity—pure potatoes, butter, cream, salt and pepper with the addition of roasted garlic. Perfect for soaking up juices of Beef Bourguignon.

3 pounds (about 4 large) white russet potatoes or Yukon Gold potatoes
4 tablespoons butter
½ to ¾ cup milk or light cream
Salt and pepper to taste
1 head roasted garlic (see p. 179 for technique)

Roasted garlic makes a slightly sweet, nutty spread that has the consistency of butter. Spread it on French bread for an appetizer or add it to mashed potatoes or soups.

1. Peel and quarter potatoes. Place in a medium saucepan and cover with water. Add ½ teaspoon salt and bring to a boil over high heat. Reduce heat and simmer potatoes until tender, about 30 minutes.

2. Drain potatoes. Heat milk in microwave in a glass measure for 30 to 60 seconds or until very hot. Mash potatoes with potato masher or run through a ricer. Add butter, ½ cup hot milk, and salt and pepper to taste. Add pulp from roasted garlic. Continue to beat until fluffy, adding additional milk as necessary to make a soft puree that just falls from the spoon. Makes 6 servings

INDIVIDUAL APPLE TARTS

I sampled many wonderful pastries while in France and apples appeared frequently in many of the desserts. This recipe is very easy to make and is so good! Although I did not detect any cinnamon in the tarts in France, I chose to include it here simply because I like it.

3 apples (Granny Smith or Jonathan)
1 to 2 tablespoons fresh lemon juice
½ cup sugar
¼ teaspoon salt
½ teaspoon cinnamon
1 sheet frozen puff pastry, thawed but chilled (prefer Pepperidge Farm)
3 tablespoons dry bread crumbs
2 to 3 tablespoons butter
Optional Garnishes: Powdered sugar, caramel sauce, ice cream or whipped cream

1. Preheat oven to 425°F. Wash, peel, core and slice apples. Place in a bowl and sprinkle with lemon juice. Combine sugar, salt and cinnamon in a small bowl; set aside.

2. Lightly roll chilled puff pasty into a rectangle just to smooth out the fold lines. Trim edges with a pizza wheel. Cut into thirds along the fold lines, and then cut each rectangle into three squares. Place pastry onto a baking pan that's been lined with parchment paper (this makes clean-up easier).

3. Sprinkle 1 teaspoon bread crumbs on each square to absorb some of the apple juices. Arrange 3 apple slices on the pastry squares in a single layer. Sprinkle generously with sugar mixture. Dot with a little butter.

4. Bake for 15 to 20 minutes in preheated oven, or until pastry is puffed and golden brown. Serve warm. Place each on a dessert plate. Garnish with powdered sugar if desired, drizzle with caramel sauce, and serve with ice cream or whipped cream. Makes 9 servings

PRIZE *Winning* LATINO DINNER

When I say prize-winning, I am not kidding. My Coco Lopez Soufflé took the Grand Prize in Borden's Coco Lopez Cream of Coconut Contest; my Toasted Chicken Quesadillas took the Grand Prize in Kikkoman's Teriyaki Recipe Contest. Both contests were open to chefs and food professionals; I entered on a lark and, surprisingly, won!   These recipes were both judged on taste, originality, presentation and ease of preparation, so rest assured they are not difficult but are delicious. Serve this winning menu to your family and friends and no doubt, you will be declared the champion!

The Toasted Chicken Quesadillas with Mango Salsa makes an exciting appetizer when served in small portions, or larger

portions may be served for a lunch treat. The Smoking Chile Pork Loin and Cranberry Jezebel Sauce are a lovely combination—the sauce adding just a little bite of jalapeno. The delicious but unusual flavor combination of the chilled Coco Lopez Soufflé provides an ideal finish to a prize-winning meal.

PRIZE WINNING LATINO DINNER

Toasted Teriyaki Chicken Quesadillas
with Mango Red Pepper Salsa

Smokin' Chile Pork Tenderloin with
Cranberry Jezebel Sauce

Vanilla Roasted Sweet Potato Wedges

Roasted Zucchini, Corn and
Chiles in Lime Butter

Coco Lopez Soufflé

A ripe mango will be soft but not squishy when gently squeezed. A very soft one is very ripe and will be too sweet and mushy. When purchased firm, let set at room temperature a few days and they will ripen nicely.

TOASTED TERIYAKI CHICKEN QUESADILLAS WITH MANGO RED PEPPER SALSA

This recipe was the Grand Prize Winner of Kikkoman's Teriyaki Contest for Culinary Professionals. I think one of the things that made my quesadillas a winning recipe was I toasted them in the oven instead of the traditional frying in a skillet. Not only is it easier but you can do a whole pan at one time, and they are toasty and contain much less fat.

4 cups coarsely chopped cooked chicken breast
6 ounces pepper jack cheese, shredded
⅓ cup Kikkoman Teriyaki Marinade and Sauce
½ cup loosely packed chopped cilantro leaves, divided use
4 10-inch soft flour tortillas
1 tablespoon butter, room temperature

Mango Red Pepper Salsa
2 cups chopped fresh mango
½ cup finely chopped red bell pepper
2 tablespoons fresh lime juice
Garnish: ½ cup sour cream (regular or light)

1. Place chicken in a large bowl; add pepper jack cheese, Kikkoman Teriyaki Marinade and Sauce, and ⅓ cup cilantro; toss to mix. Set aside.

2. Preheat oven to 400°F. Place tortillas on a flat surface. Divide chicken mixture evenly over one half of each tortilla. Fold top over the filled half. Lightly oil or line a 10 x 14-inch baking sheet with parchment paper. Place quesadillas on baking sheet and brush tops of quesadillas with softened butter. Toast in preheated oven for 9 to 12 minutes or until golden.

3. Meanwhile combine mango, red bell pepper, lime juice and remaining cilantro. Set aside.

4. To serve, cut quesadillas into 4 wedges. Serve with sour cream and Mango Red Pepper Salsa. Makes 4 quesadillas: 4 main dish servings or about 8 appetizer servings

HOW TO PEEL A MANGO:

Be careful when peeling a mango. Stand the mango on the cutting board with the stem end in your palm. Cut off each of the flat sides, or the "cheeks." Then with a paring knife, make cross-hatches in the flesh side of each of the cheeks, cutting to but not through the skin. Then turning the cut side up, slice off the pieces and you have lovely chopped mango.

SMOKIN' CHILE PORK TENDERLOIN WITH CRANBERRY JEZEBEL SAUCE

A great flavor-packed pork tenderloin brimming with Latin flair.

Seasoning
½ cup minced onion
2 garlic cloves, minced
2 to 3 teaspoons chopped chipotle chiles
   in adobo sauce, plus 1 teaspoon adobo
   sauce
2 tablespoons olive or vegetable oil
1 ½ teaspoons salt
1 teaspoon ground cumin
1 teaspoon lime zest, optional

2 pork tenderloins (1½ to 2 pounds)
1 teaspoon chili powder
½ teaspoon salt
¼ teaspoon black pepper
Garnish: Chopped chives or cilantro

1. Combine all seasoning ingredients together in a small bowl.

2. Place pork tenderloins on a cutting board. If there is a layer of silver skin, remove it with a sharp knife and discard. Pat meat dry. Cut each tenderloin vertically, not quite all the way through, to open up like a book. Spoon about 3 tablespoons of the chipotle seasoning mixture over the cut surface of the tenderloin. Roll up from the long edge like a jelly roll, seam-side down. Place on a foil-lined baking sheet. Repeat procedure with remaining tenderloin. Spread any remaining seasoning mixture over the surface of both tenderloins. Cover tightly with plastic wrap and refrigerate several hours or overnight.

3. Preheat oven to 375°F. Sprinkle tops of tenderloins with chili powder, salt and pepper. Roast tenderloins for 25 to 30 minutes or until meat registers 155°F.

4. When done, remove tenderloins from oven and tent with foil to keep warm. Let stand 15 minutes. To serve, slice tenderloins into ¾ inch slices, arranging 3 to 4 slices on each dinner plate. Serve with Cranberry Jezebel Sauce. Garnish with chives or cilantro, as desired. Makes 4 to 6 servings

Cranberry Jezebel Sauce
½ cup water
½ cup sugar
½ cup brown sugar
¼ cup lime juice
1 (10-ounce) package fresh cranberries,
   picked over

1 medium jalapeño chile, seeded and
   chopped
8 ounces (red) jalapeño pepper jelly
2 teaspoons grated lime zest
2 ripe avocados, halved, pitted and diced
¼ cup chopped fresh cilantro

In a small pan, bring water, sugars and lime juice to a boil. Add the cranberries and chopped jalapeño. Return to a boil and cook for 4 to 5 minutes or until berries pop and become tender. Add the pepper jelly and lime zest. Cover and refrigerate. Stir in avocados and cilantro before serving. Season to taste with salt and pepper. Makes about 4 cups

Mexican Rice "Risotto" page 58 also makes a nice accompaniment to this dinner.

ROASTED CORN, ZUCCHINI AND CHILES IN LIME BUTTER

Very fresh, very good and the colors are stunning!

1 (16-ounce) package frozen corn, thawed
1 medium zucchini, cut into half lengthwise, then thinly sliced horizontally
1 red bell pepper, chopped
1 jalapeño, seeded and minced
1 (15-ounce) can black beans, rinsed and drained
2 or 3 Roma tomatoes, seeded and chopped
½ medium onion, peeled and cut into thin wedges

Seasoning Mixture
3 tablespoons melted butter
1 tablespoon fresh lime juice
1 garlic clove, minced
1 teaspoon salt
¼ teaspoon black pepper

1. **Preheat** oven to 400°F. Combine vegetables in a large bowl. Melt butter; stir in lime juice, garlic, salt and pepper. Toss with vegetables. Arrange on a shallow, foiled-lined baking sheet.

2. **Roast** in preheated oven for 20 minutes or until vegetables are tender and corn appears slightly "parched". Stir occasionally during roasting. Season to taste with additional salt and pepper if desired. Makes 6 servings

VANILLA ROASTED SWEET POTATO WEDGES

3 medium sweet potatoes (about 2 pounds)
4 tablespoons butter, melted
2 teaspoons sugar
½ teaspoon vanilla extract
Salt (preferably coarse kosher salt)

Bonnie's Tip:
Pre-cooking the sweet potatoes in the microwave a few minutes first shortens the time in the oven and keeps them moist and tender.

1. **Scrub** sweet potatoes and pat dry. Make a couple of slits in each potato with a knife for steam to escape. Microwave on High for 4 to 6 minutes or just until potatoes begin to soften. Remove and set aside until cool enough to handle.

2. **Preheat** oven to 450°F. Peel potatoes and cut into thick wedges. Place in shallow bowl. Combine melted butter, sugar and vanilla. Drizzle over wedges and toss to coat. Arrange wedges on a baking sheet and roast in preheated oven for 20 minutes, or until golden. Season with kosher salt and serve. Makes 6 servings

COCO LOPEZ SOUFFLÉ

This chilled soufflé is airy, light and has the most fascinating flavor: a blend of orange, coconut and a hint of chocolate. Everyone loves it, including the panel of judges who awarded it the Grand Prize in a professional competition. Instead of chilling it in a large soufflé or trifle bowl, it could be distributed among pretty stemmed glasses for individual servings. Either way, it is a winner!

2 envelopes unflavored gelatin
½ cup cold water
4 egg yolks
¼ cup sugar
1 (15-ounce) can Coco Lopez Cream of Coconut
1 cup pineapple juice
¼ cup frozen orange juice concentrate
¼ cup clear crème de cacao liqueur
1 tablespoon lemon juice
½ teaspoon grated orange peel
3 cups heavy cream
Garnishes: Orange twists, sweetened whipped cream, shaved chocolate and fresh mint

1. Soften gelatin by stirring into water. Set aside a few minutes to soften. In a stainless steel bowl, whisk egg yolks and sugar. Set bowl over pan of hot water. Cook and stir over low heat until egg mixture becomes very hot and slightly thickened. Do not boil. Add gelatin to hot egg mixture; stir until dissolved.

2. Pour egg mixture into a large bowl. Stir in Coco Lopez Cream of Coconut, pineapple juice, orange juice concentrate, crème de cacao, lemon juice and grated orange peel into egg mixture. Stir until thoroughly combined.

3. Chill until partially set, about 45 minutes (mixture will be consistency of egg whites) stirring frequently. Mixture may be speed chilled by placing bowl containing mixture in a large pan of ice and water, stirring frequently.

4. Whip cream; beat just until it will hold soft peaks. Fold whipped cream into chilled gelatin mixture. Tape a 3-inch-aluminum foil collar around the rim of a 1 ½-quart-soufflé dish. Pour mixture into the dish; chill 8 hours or until set. Remove collar. Garnish with whipped cream, shaved chocolate, orange twist and fresh mint. Makes 8 servings

This was my first Grand Prize Winning recipe. As fate would have it, I was scheduled to teach a Mexican themed cooking class and was in a quandary as to what to make for dessert. About that same time, I received an announcement of the Coco Lopez contest for food professionals. On a whim, I hopped in the car, headed for the supermarket and purchased three cans of Coco Lopez Cream of Coconut.

This is the recipe I came up with in my kitchen. I tested it on my cooking class; they loved it! I then entered it in the contest. It made the final rounds and I traveled to the Borden's Kitchen with other contestants to make our food for the judges. No one was more surprised than I when my Coco Lopez Soufflé was announced as the Grand Prize Winner!

DINING *French Bistro* STYLE

French Bistro is typically a small neighborhood restaurant where regional, homestyle cuisine is served. Fresh seasonal ingredients are emphasized, and liberal portions are laced with robust seasonings. This menu contains hearty food made to be shared in typical French bistro fashion—friends gathered around a table, savoring good food and enjoying lively conversation.

Prepare this menu on a day when you will enjoy puttering around the kitchen, as it will take time for the foods to cook. The onions must  be caramelized for the French Onion Soup—a step that should not be hurried. The chicken requires time in the oven to roast until it is golden and crispy, and the Potatoes Dauphinoise require baking in a rich sauce until they have melded into a gratin. However, you will be richly rewarded with fragrant aromas filling the air and French Bistro fare on the table.

DINING FRENCH BISTRO STYLE

French Onion Soup

Roast Chicken with Herb Butter,
Carrots and Onions

Potatoes Dauphinoise

Pot de Crème with White Chocolate
Whipped Cream

FRENCH ONION SOUP

A great onion soup, easy to make and one that you will want to serve time and again. This has been a cooking class favorite over the years.

½ cup butter
2 ½ pounds yellow onions, halved, and sliced ¼ inch thick (8 cups)
½ teaspoon dried thyme
½ cup sherry
3 cups chicken broth
3 cups beef broth
Salt and black pepper
French baguette, sliced (⅓ inch thick)
2 ⅔ cups grated Gruyere cheese
Optional garnish: Fresh thyme leaves

The rich flavor of the soup results from caramelizing the onions. Cook the onions slowly until the sugars turn a deep, rich golden brown. Then deglazing the pan with the sherry enhances the flavor of this beautiful soup.

1. In a large saucepan or Dutch oven, add butter and melt over medium heat. Add the onions and lower the heat to medium low. Add thyme and cook, stirring frequently, until the onions start to turn golden brown, about 25 minutes.

2. Add the sherry and cook until the sherry is almost completely evaporated and the onions are brown, about 15 minutes.

3. Add the broths and bring to a boil. Lower the heat and simmer for 30 minutes. Season to taste with salt and pepper.

4. Preheat the oven to 450°F. Ladle the soup into eight ovenproof soup bowls. Place the soup bowls on a sheet pan. Cover the top of the soup with a slice of French bread. Top each bowl with ⅓ cup cheese. Place in the oven and bake until the cheese is golden brown and bubbly, about 10 minutes.
Makes 8 servings

ROAST CHICKEN WITH HERB BUTTER, CARROTS AND ONIONS

Julia Child once said you can tell whether someone is a good cook by how they roast a chicken. With this recipe, you will be well on your way to success!

1 (4-pound) chicken
Salt and pepper
½ lemon
1 head garlic, cut in half crosswise
1 rib celery
2 tablespoons (¼ stick) butter, melted
½ teaspoon thyme
2 cloves garlic
1 large yellow onion, cut into wedges
4 carrots cut into 2-inch chunks (or 1 pound baby carrots)
Olive oil
Garnish: Fresh thyme sprigs

1. **Preheat** the oven to 425°F. Remove the chicken giblets. Rinse the chicken inside and out. Remove any excess fat and leftover pin feathers and pat the outside dry.

2. **Liberally** salt and pepper the inside of the chicken. Stuff the cavity with lemon half, garlic and celery. Combine melted butter with thyme and garlic. Brush the outside of the chicken with the butter mixture and sprinkle again with salt and pepper. Tie the legs together with kitchen string and tuck the wing tips under the body of the chicken.

Bonnie's Tip:
Allowing the roasted chicken to rest for 20 minutes before slicing makes a more tender roast chicken. Resting allows the juices to stabilize and be reabsorbed by the flesh instead of running out on the plate.

3. **Place** the onions and carrots in a roasting pan. Season with salt and pepper and toss with olive oil. Spread around the bottom of the roasting pan; add ½ cup water and place the chicken on top.

4. **Roast** the chicken, uncovered, for 1 ½ hours, or until the juices run clear when you cut between a leg and thigh.

5. **Remove** the chicken and vegetables to a platter and cover with aluminum foil for about 20 minutes. Slice the chicken and serve it with the vegetables. Makes 4 to 6 servings

POTATOES DAUPHINOISE

Oh, how good this is! I like to make it with Gruyere cheese, which has a delectable flavor and melts beautifully. However, other cheeses may be used; Swiss is a good one as well.

2 ¼ cups heavy cream
1 3-inch sprig fresh thyme
2 garlic cloves, minced
⅛ teaspoon grated fresh nutmeg
Butter
3 ½ pounds Yukon Gold potatoes, peeled and sliced ⅛-inch thick
Salt and freshly ground black pepper
8 ounces Gruyere or Swiss cheese, shredded
½ cup grated Parmesan cheese, plus 3 tablespoons more for top
Garnish: Fresh thyme (optional)

Bonnie's Tip:
To get beautiful, square servings as pictured, allow the potatoes to cool awhile as indicated. Then, using a square cutter with an open top, cut straight down into the potatoes. Slide a spatula under the cut serving and lift it out onto the plate, sliding the spatula out from the bottom and lifting the cutter off the top. Repeat with remaining servings.

1. Preheat the oven to 375°F. In a saucepan, warm cream with thyme, garlic and nutmeg.

2. Butter a 9 x 13-inch-baking pan. Layer one-third of potatoes in an overlapping pattern and season with salt and pepper. Remove cream from heat, then pour ¾ cup over the potatoes.

3. Sprinkle a third of the cheese over the potatoes. Repeat with second and third layers. Bake, uncovered, for 45 minutes or until potatoes are very tender. Cover with foil if potatoes are browning too quickly. Let rest for 15 minutes; then sprinkle with Parmesan cheese and put under broiler to brown top. Makes 8 to 10 servings

POT DE CRÈME WITH WHITE CHOCOLATE WHIPPED CREAM

Rich, dense and chocolaty—just what you would expect from this exquisite French dessert!

2 cups heavy cream
½ cup milk
¾ cup bittersweet chocolate chips
5 egg yolks
⅓ cup granulated sugar
1 teaspoon vanilla extract
Pinch salt
White Chocolate Whipped Cream (recipe follows)
Garnish: Grated chocolate

1. Place oven rack in center position and preheat oven to 375°F. Place cream and milk in microwave-safe container and microwave on High 1 to 1 ½ minutes, or until mixture is very hot but not boiling. Remove from heat. Stir in chocolate chips; whisk until melted.

2. In a medium mixing bowl, whisk together the egg yolks, sugar, vanilla and salt until the sugar is completely dissolved. Slowly whisk the hot cream mixture into the egg mixture. (If you add the hot cream mixture too quickly, the egg yolks could cook and leave undesirable cooked egg particles.) Pour the hot mixture through a fine mesh strainer.

3. Ladle mixture into 6 (¾-cup) ramekins. Place filled ramekins in a baking pan with 1 ½ inch-high-sides. Pour enough hot water into baking pan to reach halfway up the sides of the ramekins. Bake until mixture around the edges of the ramekin is firm when lightly shaken, about 35 minutes. (Baking time will vary depending on depth and width of ramekins.) The center of the Pots de Crème may still jiggle slightly when shaken, but that is okay, as they will firm up as they chill.

4. Carefully remove the ramekins from the baking pan, wipe dry and allow to cool. Cover and refrigerate until firm, about 2 to 3 hours. To serve, garnish with White Chocolate Whipped Cream and garnish with grated chocolate. Makes 6 servings

White Chocolate Whipped Cream
2 ounces white chocolate, finely chopped
1 ½ cups heavy cream, chilled
1 teaspoon vanilla extract

Melt the white chocolate in a double boiler over barely simmering water, stirring occasionally. Once melted, remove from heat and cool to room temperature. Whip the cream in a chilled bowl to very soft peaks. Fold in the cooled chocolate and vanilla. Pipe or spoon the whipped cream onto desserts.

Bonnie's Tip:
For best results when whipping cream, chill the bowl and beaters and be sure the cream is adequately chilled for best volume.

To safely handle ramekins in a hot water bath, place the pan with ramekins in the oven and then pour hot water around the ramekins until it reaches half way up the sides of the ramekins. It is much safer than carrying a pan of hot water to the oven.

DINNER at the INN

When I need a short retreat from a hectic schedule, I love to take a leisurely drive though the country, perhaps venturing down a winding road with trees blazing with colors and soaking up the beautiful scenery. My short getaways usually include dinner at a country inn as the final destination, where the atmosphere is warm and comfy and the dining delectable.

Whether or not you actually have dinner at the inn, you can enjoy comfort foods typically served there with this menu. The Sherried Mushroom, Ham and Wild Rice Soup would make a great lunch on its own. The Marinated Thick Pork Chops with Pan Sauce might be the best pork chops you have ever had and do try the Broccoli with Toasted Garlic Crumbs. And to put the meal over the top, finish with the White Chocolate Banana Cream Pie in Almond Crust.

DINNER AT THE INN

Sherried Mushroom, Ham
and Wild Rice Soup

Marinated Thick Pork Chops
with Pan Sauce

Broccoli with Toasted Garlic Crumbs

Pike County Fried Apples

White Chocolate Banana Cream Pie
in Almond Crust

SHERRIED MUSHROOM, HAM AND WILD RICE SOUP

A very nice soup to warm both body and soul. The thyme and sherry give this a wonderful flavor.

⅓ cup butter
1 cup sliced mushrooms
1 tablespoon minced onion
½ cup flour
3 cups chicken broth
2 cups cooked wild rice
1 cup chopped cooked ham
¼ cup shredded carrots
½ teaspoon dried thyme
½ teaspoon salt
1 cup half-and-half
3 tablespoons dry sherry
Garnish: Chopped chives

1. Melt butter in saucepan over medium heat. Sauté mushrooms and onion until tender. Blend in flour. Cook for a minute or two until bubbly.

2. Whisk in broth. Cook, stirring constantly, until mixture comes to a boil. Simmer for 1 minute, stirring constantly. Stir in rice, ham, carrots, thyme and salt. Simmer 2 minutes.

3. Whisk in half-and-half and sherry; heat to simmer. To serve, ladle into bowls and garnish with chives. Makes 4 to 6 servings

PIKE COUNTY FRIED APPLES

I grew up in Pike County, only a few miles from the renowned Stark Orchards, one of the country's foremost producers of good apple stock. My dad had numerous fruit trees from Stark planted in the orchard, many of which were dwarf or double-dwarf varieties. In the fall, we enjoyed apples in many forms. Fried apples often appeared along with pork chops and even sometimes for breakfasts, when my mom would serve them with homemade sausage patties and freshly baked biscuits. I think you will enjoy them, too.

4 medium Jonathan, Granny Smith or Gala apples (or other good cooking apple)
2 tablespoons butter
¼ cup sugar
Pinch salt

1. **Wash** apples and cut in half. Remove core, stem and blossom ends. Cut into thin slices. (If prepping ahead, soak in a bowl of cold water with ¼ cup lemon juice added. Drain well and pat dry with paper towel before proceeding with recipe.)

2. **In** a large skillet, heat the butter until bubbling. Add the apple slices to the skillet and continue to cook over medium-high heat for approximately 5 minutes or until tender-crisp and beginning to brown. Turn several times to brown evenly.

3. **Add** the sugar and pinch of salt; continue to cook until sugar has melted and started to caramelize. Apple slices should be tender. Serve warm. Makes 4 servings

BROCCOLI WITH TOASTED GARLIC CRUMBS

You will not believe how good broccoli can be with this treatment. To get my family to eat broccoli, it must have cheese! With or without the cheese, this broccoli dish provides a savory crunch. Panko (Japanese bread crumbs) provides extra crunch and may be found in most supermarkets with Asian ingredients or with regular bread crumbs.

1 pound broccoli florets
½ teaspoon salt
3 tablespoons butter
1 garlic clove, minced

½ cup panko
Pinch of salt
1 cup shredded Cheddar or Monterey
   Jack cheese

1. **Put** 1 inch of water in a 3-quart pot. Place a steamer basket inside and bring water to a boil. Add broccoli; sprinkle with salt, cover and steam until just tender, 6 to 8 minutes.

2. **Meanwhile,** make the toasted panko crumb topping. Melt butter in a skillet over moderately low heat; add minced garlic, stirring occasionally, until fragrant. Do not burn! Stir in the panko and salt; increase heat to moderate and cook, stirring occasionally, until crumbs are golden, about 2 to 3 minutes.

3. **Remove** steamer basket, empty water from the pot. Return broccoli to warm pot and add shredded cheese, tossing to mix so cheese melts from the heat of the broccoli. Transfer to a shallow serving dish and spoon toasted panko crumbs over the top. Makes 4 servings

MARINATED THICK PORK CHOPS WITH PAN SAUCE

Brining these pork chops for two days results in succulent, tender meat. Brining is not difficult, but plan ahead for these tender, creamy chops!

Brine
3 cups water
4 large garlic cloves, minced
¼ cup kosher salt
3 tablespoons black peppercorns
3 tablespoons sugar
2 teaspoons dried thyme, crumbled
½ teaspoon ground allspice
1 bay leaf

6 (1 ½-inch-thick) rib pork chops
4 tablespoons light brown sugar, firmly
   packed
1 ½ teaspoons kosher salt
¼ teaspoon ground red pepper
3 tablespoons vegetable oil

Pan Sauce
3 tablespoons flour
2 ½ cups half-and-half or milk
Garnish: Fresh thyme or chives

1. Make Brine: Bring water to a boil. Add all the brine ingredients and simmer for 5 minutes. Stir ice into the brine to cool it quickly. If you do not have 1 ½ quarts of liquid, add enough cool water to make 1 ½ quarts.

2. Place pork chops in a large zipper top bag or other container. Add brine and seal; refrigerate for 24 to 48 hours. If chops are not completely covered with brine, turn them occasionally while marinating.

3. In a small bowl, mix together brown sugar, kosher salt and ground red pepper. Remove pork chops from brine, discarding brine and any spices still adhering to chops; pat dry. Sprinkle each side of each chop with about 1 teaspoon of the brown sugar mixture, patting it into the meat.

4. Cook Chops: Heat a sauté pan over medium-high heat; add oil. Add chops and brown on each side; transfer to a baking sheet. Roast chops in preheated 450°F oven, about 10 minutes, or until meat thermometer registers 155°F. Transfer chops to a platter and let stand 5 minutes before serving.

5. For the Pan Sauce: While chops are finishing in the oven, make the pan sauce. You should have about 3 tablespoons oil remaining in the skillet. If not, add a bit more to make 3 tablespoons. Stir flour into the pan and stir to mix with pan drippings. Heat to bubbling and cook for 30 to 60 seconds.

6. Add the half-and-half to the flour mixture and stir to completely combine. Cook over medium heat, stirring constantly until mixture comes to a boil. Reduce heat and simmer until mixture thickens to desired consistency. (If it becomes too thick, add a little milk or water to thin it down.) Season to taste with salt and pepper.

7. To serve, drizzle sauce over chops and garnish with fresh thyme sprigs or chives.
Makes 6 servings

For brining, use coarse-grained kosher salt. For baking use fine-grained salt because it dissolves easily. There are several very nice sea salts available; they come in coarse or fine grind. Sea salt has a very clean, fresh taste and contains no additives. Usually, I use it for finishing dishes, sprinkling a little on before serving.

Bonnie's Tip:
When melting chocolate in the microwave, chop pieces very fine and place in a dry glass measure. Microwave on High for 30 seconds; remove and stir. If not warm enough, use 15 second intervals to heat chocolate, stirring each time. Chocolate holds its shape and you cannot tell by looking whether it has melted or not; you must stir it. Chocolate does not need to be hot, just warm enough to melt with stirring.

WHITE CHOCOLATE BANANA CREAM PIE IN ALMOND CRUST

A wonderful version of an old favorite—dressed up for the evening with a delectable almond crust and with the addition of white chocolate!

Crust
½ cup butter, room temperature
¼ cup sugar
1 extra large egg, beaten to blend
1 ⅓ cups all-purpose flour
⅔ cup finely chopped, toasted almonds
¼ teaspoon baking powder
⅛ teaspoon salt

Filling
3 large egg yolks
2 cups milk
⅔ cup granulated sugar
¼ cup cornstarch
Pinch of salt
2 teaspoons vanilla extract
3 ounces white chocolate, coarsely chopped
3 medium bananas, thinly sliced (about 1/4 inch thick)

Topping
2 ounces white chocolate, coarsely chopped
1 ½ cups heavy cream, chilled
¼ cup powdered sugar
1 teaspoon vanilla extract

Garnish: 1 ounce white chocolate, shaved

1. For the Crust: Cream butter and sugar in food processor until smooth and fluffy. Add egg and blend until smooth. Add flour, almonds, baking power and salt and process until just combined. Gather dough into a ball, then flatten into a disk. Wrap in plastic and refrigerate for 1 hour. (May be done up to 2 days in advance.)

2. Roll out dough between plastic wrap into a 10 ½ inch circle. Transfer dough into 9-inch-diameter glass pie dish, trimming excess if necessary. Turn under overhang and crimp edge decoratively. Refrigerate 1 hour. Bake at 375°F for 15 minutes or until golden brown. Cool.

3. For the Filling: In a medium bowl, whisk the egg yolks with milk and transfer to a heavy 3-quart saucepan. In a small bowl, combine the sugar, cornstarch and salt, mixing well; whisk into the egg and milk mixture. Cook over medium heat, whisking constantly, until the custard is thickened and comes to a boil. Stir in vanilla.

4. Remove from heat and add chopped white chocolate; stir until melted.

5. To assemble the Pie: Slice bananas into the baked pie shell, covering the bottom. Spoon the custard over the bananas. Press a piece of plastic wrap over filling and refrigerate until chilled, about 2 hours.

6. For the Topping: Melt the chopped white chocolate in a microwave-safe glass measure in the microwave on High for 30 seconds; stir. If not melted, microwave on High at 15 second intervals until the chocolate is warm enough to melt upon stirring. Cool to room temperature.

7. In a large bowl, beat the cream with powdered sugar until soft peaks form. Stir in vanilla. Gently whisk one third of the whipped cream into the melted white chocolate. Then fold the white chocolate mixture into the remaining whipped cream until just combined.

8. Discard the plastic wrap from the pie. Swirl the whipped cream over the filling. Garnish with white chocolate shavings. Refrigerate until serving time. Makes one 9-inch pie

Bonnie's Tip:
To make chocolate shavings or small curls, use a vegetable peeler and run it along the edge of a chocolate bar. Carefully place the curls strategically on the pie, using a small spatula or even a toothpick.

SICILIAN
Pasta PARTY

A great party idea that virtually everyone will love! The menu can be easily doubled or even tripled for a large group. I have been making these recipes for years, as they are family favorites. Now I am still making them for my grandchildren!

Since much of this menu can be made a day or so in advance, it makes great entertaining fare. The red sauces, so much a part of Sicilian cuisine, are rich with tomatoes, laced with herbs and slowly simmered. If you have never oven-roasted meatballs, you are going to love this method. No more grease splatters on the cook top to clean up and no more browning in batches. The Vanilla Bean Panna Cotta is a lovely finish to the meal; it is creamy, light and, as my favorite Italian chef, Chef Claudio, would say, "Perfecto!"

SICILIAN PASTA PARTY

Sicilian Garden Salad
with Italian Vinaigrette

Crusty Garlic Cheese Herb Bread

Toasted Ravioli with Spicy Red Sauce

Oven Roasted Italian Meatballs in
Long-Simmered Ragu Sauce

Vanilla Bean Panna Cotta
with Honey Berry Sauce

SICILIAN GARDEN SALAD WITH ITALIAN VINAIGRETTE

This salad calls for pepperoncini, also called Tuscan peppers. They range from slightly sweet to hot, and are most often sold pickled and used as part of an antipasto.

Italian Vinaigrette
½ cup mayonnaise (prefer Hellmann's)
¼ cup white wine vinegar
2 tablespoons honey
¼ cup grated Romano cheese
1 garlic clove, minced
½ teaspoon Italian Seasoning
2 tablespoons chopped fresh parsley, optional

Salad
8 cups bite-sized salad greens (prefer Romaine lettuce), washed and dried
4 slices red onion, separated into rings
¼ cup pitted black olives
2 to 4 pepperoncini peppers
½ cup grape tomatoes, halved
½ cup croutons
Garnish: Freshly grated Romano or Parmesan cheese

1. To make Italian Vinaigrette: Place all ingredients in bowl. Whisk together until well blended.

2. To assemble Salad: Place lettuce in salad bowl. Add red onion rings, black olives, pepperoncini, tomatoes and croutons. Add plenty of Italian Vinaigrette and toss. Sprinkle freshly grated Parmesan cheese over the top and serve. Makes 4 to 6 servings

Bonnie's Tip:
Italian Seasoning is a blend of herbs used in Italian cooking. If you don't have that, substitute ¼ teaspoon oregano and ¼ teaspoon basil for the ½ teaspoon Italian seasoning.

TOASTED RAVIOLI WITH SPICY RED SAUCE

Toasted Ravioli originated on "The Hill"—an Italian section of St. Louis, Missouri. Ravioli is fried and served as an appetizer with a richly spiced tomato sauce for dipping.

2 large eggs
½ cup half-and-half
1 cup Italian-style bread crumbs
¼ teaspoon salt
Vegetable oil for frying
24 fresh or frozen bite-size, cheese ravioli (if using frozen, thaw first)
¼ cup freshly grated Parmesan cheese
Spicy Red Sauce, recipe follows

1. In a shallow bowl beat together eggs and half-and-half. Put bread crumbs and salt in another shallow bowl. Dip ravioli in egg mixture to coat, letting excess drip off, and dredge in bread crumbs, knocking off excess. Arrange ravioli on a tray.

2. In a heavy skillet, heat 2 inches oil over moderate heat to 350°F. With a slotted spoon gently lower a few ravioli into oil; do not crowd. Fry, turning them occasionally, until golden brown and cooked through, about 2 to 3 minutes. Transfer ravioli with slotted spoon to paper towels to drain. Return oil to 350°F before frying remaining ravioli in same manner.

3. Transfer hot ravioli to a platter and sprinkle with Parmesan. Serve ravioli with warm Spicy Red Sauce for dipping. Makes 4 to 6 appetizer servings

Spicy Red Sauce
3 tablespoons olive oil
1 medium onion, chopped
3 garlic cloves, minced
1 green pepper, chopped
1 (16-ounce) can crushed tomatoes
1 (8-ounce) can tomato sauce
1 (6-ounce) can tomato paste
½ cup dry red wine
1 tablespoon dried basil
2 teaspoons dried oregano
1 teaspoon sugar
½ teaspoon thyme leaves
½ teaspoon salt
½ teaspoon black pepper
½ teaspoon crushed red pepper
¼ cup freshly grated Parmesan cheese

1. Heat olive oil, onion, garlic and green pepper in large saucepan. Cook until tender.

2. Add remaining ingredients except Parmesan cheese; bring to a boil. Reduce temperature and simmer for 30 minutes. Stir in Parmesan cheese. Serve warm with Toasted Ravioli.

Bonnie's Tip:
This is an excellent sauce. However, if time does not permit you to make it, there are some very good ones on the market that would work as well. The ones laden with herbs or those that are spicy with crushed red pepper would be the better choices.

Bonnie's Tip:
When I was in Italy, I noticed that the Italian chef always added some of the sauce to the cooked pasta. The pasta soaked up some of the flavor and didn't clump together. At serving time, he would add the remaining sauce to the dish. Since then, I have adopted his method.

OVEN-ROASTED ITALIAN MEATBALLS IN LONG-SIMMERED RAGU SAUCE

Usually I serve this with spaghetti, but penne or rotini pasta also work well. The sauce needs to be made first. It may be made in advance—the flavors blend together and it is wonderful! Just remember to cool it down quickly in a cold water bath and refrigerate. Usually, when making a lot of meatballs, I find it easier to roast them in the oven instead of browning them in hot oil. It is quicker, not as messy and uses less fat. I use lean beef and add a little extra olive oil so the meatballs will be moist.

Ragu Sauce
2 tablespoons olive oil
1 medium onion, chopped
3 cloves garlic, minced
1 (15-ounce) can tomato sauce
1 (28-ounce) can crushed tomatoes
1 (6-ounce) can tomato paste
1 cup beef or chicken broth
½ cup dry red wine
1 tablespoon dried basil leaves
2 teaspoons dried leaf oregano
2 teaspoons sugar
1 teaspoon salt
½ teaspoon dried leaf thyme
1 bay leaf
¼ teaspoon freshly ground black pepper

Meatballs
1 ½ pounds ground beef (90 percent lean)
2 eggs, slightly beaten
½ cup dry Italian-style bread crumbs
1 tablespoon olive oil
2 tablespoons minced fresh parsley
2 tablespoons grated Parmesan cheese
2 tablespoons dry white wine
1 garlic clove, minced
1 teaspoon salt
½ teaspoon black pepper
½ teaspoon dried leaf oregano
½ teaspoon dried basil leaves

1 pound spaghetti or pasta of choice
Garnish: Grated Parmesan cheese

1. For the Ragu Sauce: Place oil in a large, heavy pot with onion and garlic over medium heat. Cook, stirring frequently, until tender. Add remaining ingredients.

2. Bring to a boil; reduce heat to low and simmer, uncovered for 1 hour, stirring occasionally. Makes about 1 ¾ quarts sauce.

3. For the Meatballs: Place ground beef, eggs, bread crumbs and olive oil in a large mixing bowl. Combine to mix thoroughly. Add remaining ingredients and gently mix into meat mixture. (Clean hands are good tools here!) Form mixture into 1 ½ inch meatballs.

4. Place raw meat balls on a foil or parchment paper-lined jelly roll pan or rimmed baking sheet. Bake in 350°F oven for 20 to 30 minutes or until browned. Drop a few at a time into hot Ragu Sauce and simmer for 10 minutes. Serve over hot, cooked pasta.

5. To serve pasta with Meatballs and Ragu Sauce: Meanwhile, cook pasta according to package directions. Drain thoroughly. Stir about a cup of Ragu Sauce into the pasta,

6. Place hot cooked pasta on a large serving platter. Spoon meatballs and sauce over pasta. Sprinkle with additional Parmesan cheese if desired. Makes 6 to 8 servings

CRUSTY GARLIC CHEESE HERB BREAD

Split a loaf of commercial Italian or French bread horizontally, then spread with Garlic Cheese Herb Butter and place in a 350°F oven until the bread is toasty and the butter melts. Great with pasta or salad.

Garlic Cheese Herb Butter
1 cup butter, room temperature
½ cup grated Parmesan cheese
2 tablespoons minced fresh parsley
2 cloves garlic, minced
½ teaspoon dried marjoram
½ teaspoon dried oregano leaves
½ teaspoon dried basil leaves

In a small deep mixer bowl, whip butter until creamy and light. Add remaining ingredients, beat on medium speed until well blended. Makes 1 cup

Bonnie's Tip:
If you have any of the Garlic Cheese Herb Butter left over, use it to season vegetables. Sometimes I make extra and freeze as a quick way to give vegetables or pasta a lift.

VANILLA BEAN PANNA COTTA WITH HONEY BERRY SAUCE

Panna cotta means "cooked cream" in Italian. It is so easy to make and literally melts in the mouth. It is the epitome of easy elegance.

Panna Cotta
2 ½ teaspoons unflavored gelatin
2 cups heavy cream
1 cup half-and-half
¾ cup sugar
1 (6-inch) vanilla bean

Honey Berry Sauce
2 cups frozen unsweetened raspberries, blackberries or strawberries
   (or a mixture of all three), defrosted
2 tablespoons honey
1 tablespoon sugar
1 teaspoon fresh lemon juice

Optional Garnishes: Fresh berries, toasted sliced almonds or whipped cream

1. For the Panna Cotta: Pour ¼ cup cold water into a 1 cup glass measure or custard cup. Sprinkle with gelatin. Let stand until softened, about 4 or 5 minutes.

2. Mix cream, half-and-half and sugar in heavy large saucepan. Split vanilla bean and scrape out seeds; stir it into cream mixture. Add the vanilla pod also. Bring to a boil, stirring frequently. (This step may be done in the microwave. Place mixture in a Pyrex batter bowl and microwave on High for 4 to 5 minutes or until mixture just comes to a boil.) Remove from heat; stir gelatin mixture into hot cream. Let stand 5 minutes for the vanilla bean to steep. Strain. Divide pudding among six custard cups. Cover and refrigerate overnight.

3. For the Honey Berry Sauce: Combine berries of choice in food processor or blender. Puree. Strain into a glass measure. Stir in honey, sugar and lemon juice. Cover and chill until ready for service. (May be made up to three days in advance, covered and chilled.)

4. To serve, top Panna Cotta with Honey Berry Sauce. Garnish.
Makes 6 (5-ounce) servings

Bonnie's Tip:
Unflavored gelatin is available in our supermarkets as a dry powder and is packaged in small amounts, roughly a tablespoon. I always measure the gelatin because ½ teaspoon would make a big difference in the consistency of the recipe. Too much and it is rubbery; too little and it does not thicken. Gelatin is dissolved in a cool liquid to soften, then is usually heated in some manner to fully dissolve it and unleash its thickening power.

Casual **Fall** BUFFET

When autumn leaves float to the ground, mums burst into vibrant colors, and cool days are followed by chilly nights—fall has arrived. Along with fall come many opportunities for gatherings and this buffet would be ideal for many events, i.e. game day, a "come-on-over" invitation, home movie night, neighborhood party or simply to enjoy in front of a cozy fire.

How I love this kind of menu. No fuss, not much trouble but tastes so good. I simply adore making a great pot of chili—leftovers are always in demand. This hearty fare is guaranteed to please the guys as well as the gals. The Turtle Bars can be made a few days ahead; they are good keepers as long as you stay out of them!

CASUAL FALL BUFFET

Warm Monterrey Pepper Jack Dip

Southwest Chopped Salad

Bonnie's Quick and Easy Chili

Cornbread Wedges with
Scallions and Bacon

Turtle Bars

SOUTHWEST CHOPPED SALAD

Just about the perfect salad when friends gather for the big game. Both salad and dressing may be made in advance and combined before serving.

4 cups chopped Romaine lettuce
1 (15 ½ ounce) can black beans, rinsed and well drained
¾ cup sliced grape tomatoes
1 cup frozen corn kernels, thawed
1 avocado, diced
1 red bell pepper, chopped
¼ cup sliced green onions
1 cup coarsely crushed tortilla chips

Honey Lime Dressing
¼ cup fresh lime juice
¼ cup olive oil
2 tablespoons honey
2 tablespoons finely chopped fresh cilantro (or more to taste)
1 garlic clove, minced
½ small jalapeño pepper, seeded and minced
Garnish: Shredded Cheddar cheese

1. Toss all salad ingredients in a large bowl.

2. In separate bowl, mix dressing ingredients. Pour dressing over salad mixture and toss again. Season with salt and pepper. Garnish with shredded cheese and serve.
Makes 6 servings

CORNBREAD WEDGES WITH SCALLIONS AND BACON

A fragrant, moist cornbread that I think tastes best when baked in a hot cast iron skillet, but other hot skillets will work too. The onion and bacon make it yummy!

1 tablespoon vegetable oil
1 cup flour
1 cup yellow corn meal
¼ cup sugar
2 teaspoons baking powder
1 teaspoon salt

1 ¼ cups milk
1 large egg
⅓ cup vegetable oil
¼ cup thinly sliced scallions
2 slices bacon, cooked crisp and
   crumbled

1. Heat the oven to 400°F. Pour about 1 tablespoon oil in 10-inch skillet and place in oven to get very hot. Meanwhile, in a large bowl, whisk the flour, corn meal, sugar, baking powder, and salt. Set aside.

2. Whisk milk, egg, oil and scallions together until well combined.

3. Pour milk and egg mixture into the dry ingredients and stir with a rubber spatula until the ingredients are just blended. Fold in bacon.

4. Pour the batter into the hot skillet and bake 20 to 25 minutes or until the top is golden brown and a toothpick inserted in the center comes out clean. Cool in pan on cooling rack for 5 minutes. Turn out and cut into wedges and serve warm. Makes 8 to 10 servings

Bonnie's Tip:
Scallions are green onions, and the terms are often used interchangably in recipes.

WARM PEPPER JACK DIP

This can all be assembled ahead of time and be ready to go into the oven. Serve with tortilla chips and get the party started.

1 (8-ounce) package cream cheese, softened
⅔ cup sour cream
⅓ cup mayonnaise (prefer Hellmann's)
2 teaspoons chili powder
½ teaspoon chipotle chili powder (more or less to taste)
8 ounces shredded pepper jack cheese (some brands labeled Monterrey pepper jack)
1 small minced jalapeño, optional
3 green onions, finely chopped
¼ cup chopped cilantro
Tortilla chips for dipping

1. Preheat oven to 350°F. Stir together all ingredients in a bowl until well mixed. Spoon into a buttered 8-inch au gratin dish.

2. Bake for 30 minutes or until bubbly. Garnish if desired with cilantro sprigs and serve with tortilla chips.

BONNIE'S QUICK AND EASY CHILI

Although this chili is made quickly, the flavor will be better if allowed to simmer for a longer period of time. Also, if you like more beans, feel free to add another can.

1 tablespoon vegetable oil
2 pounds ground beef
1 onion, chopped
3 cloves garlic, minced
1 or 2 jalapeños, seeded and chopped
¼ cup chili powder
1 tablespoon ground cumin
1 tablespoon unsweetened cocoa (prefer Hershey's), optional

2 teaspoons salt
½ teaspoon black pepper
1 cup beef broth
1 (15-ounce) can crushed tomatoes
2 (16-ounce) cans chili beans with sauce
1 (10 ¾-ounce) can cream of tomato soup
¼ cup chopped cilantro
Garnish: Sour cream, shredded Cheddar cheese and/or tortilla chips

Bonnie's Tip:
Sometimes after browning the beef, I put all remaining ingredients into the crockpot and let it simmer on low for 6 to 8 hours.

Or, it may be made in advance, cooled down quickly in a cold water bath, and then refrigerated overnight. Put in the crockpot the next day on a slow simmer for serving later in the day.

1. Place vegetable oil in 6-quart-Dutch oven over medium heat. Add ground beef and cook, stirring and breaking up any clumps, for 6 to 7 minutes or until no longer pink.

2. Add onion, garlic, and jalapeños to the pan and cook until vegetables are softened. Stir in the chili powder, cumin, cocoa, salt and pepper; mixing well into the meat mixture. Cook for a minute or two for the flavors to blend.

3. Add beef broth and bring the chili mixture to a boil; simmer for a couple of minutes. Add the tomatoes, beans and tomato soup; bring to a boil. Reduce heat, cover and simmer at least for 15 minutes. Simmer longer over low heat if desired to allow flavors to blend, stirring occasionally. Stir in cilantro before serving. Ladle into bowls and garnish as desired. Makes 10 to 12 servings

TURTLE BARS

If you like pecan pie, you are going to love these bars! They are rich, dense and delectable, with a dark chocolate layer between the base and the pecan topping.

Cookie Base
1 cup plus 2 tablespoons cold butter, cut into ½ inch pieces
3 cups flour
¾ cup packed light brown sugar, firmly packed
1 tablespoon ground cinnamon
¾ teaspoon salt
½ cup semi-sweet or bittersweet chocolate chips

Pecan Topping
3 cups pecans
¾ cups butter
1 ½ cup packed brown sugar, firmly packed
½ cup honey
3 tablespoons heavy cream
¾ teaspoon salt

1. For the Cookie Base: Position oven rack in the center position and preheat oven to 350°F. Place the butter, flour, brown sugar, cinnamon, and salt in food processor fitted with metal blade. Pulse about 20 times, until butter is cut into mixture evenly.

2. Press mixture firmly into bottom of a 9 x 13-inch-baking pan. Bake until firm and lightly browned, about 20 minutes. When the cookie base comes out of the oven, sprinkle the chocolate chips evenly over the top. (Don't turn off the oven.) Set the pan aside for chocolate chips to soften. Then smooth over cookie base to make a chocolate layer.

3. For the Pecan Topping: As the cookie base bakes, pulse the pecans in the food processor until coarsely chopped. In a 2-quart, heavy saucepan, melt the butter. Stir in the brown sugar, honey, cream, and salt. Simmer for 1 minute, stirring occasionally. Mix in pecans. Pour the pecan mixture over the chocolate coated cookie base; spread evenly.

4. Bake 15 to 18 minutes or until the filling is bubbling. Let cool completely in the pan. When ready to serve, cut into 1 ½ or 2 inch squares. Makes a 9 x13-inch pan

AUTUMN
Country Road

Taking an autumn road trip along the back country roads, watching Fall unfold around you, renews the spirit and whets the appetite for the aromas and foods of harvest. This menu, composed of the colors and vibrant flavors of Fall, showcases the rich culinary heritage of our land.

This menu speaks of Fall—butternut squash made into a creamy soup, a chicken beautifully smoked, and cranberries combined with dried apricots to create a fabulous side dish. Comforting warm desserts are in order and the Hot Lemon Soufflés drenched with raspberry sauce certainly fills the bill.

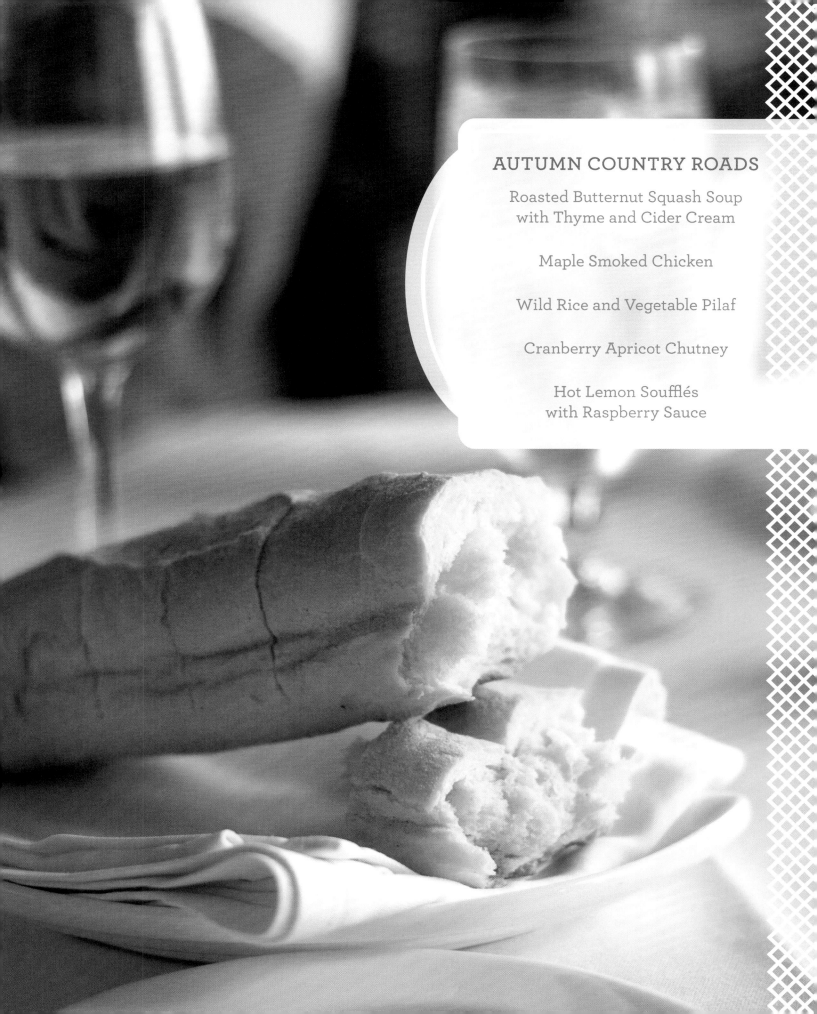

AUTUMN COUNTRY ROADS

Roasted Butternut Squash Soup
with Thyme and Cider Cream

Maple Smoked Chicken

Wild Rice and Vegetable Pilaf

Cranberry Apricot Chutney

Hot Lemon Soufflés
with Raspberry Sauce

ROASTED BUTTERNUT SQUASH SOUP WITH THYME AND CIDER CREAM

This is a very pretty presentation. The soup may be made ahead, chilled and reheated before serving. The Cider Cream may be made 24 hours in advance.

¼ cup butter
1 medium onion, chopped
½ cup chopped peeled carrot
½ cup chopped celery
3 pounds butternut squash, roasted
1 tart apple (Granny Smith or Jonathan), peeled, cored, chopped
1 ½ teaspoons dried thyme

½ teaspoon crumbled dried sage leaves
¼ teaspoon ground ginger, optional
5 ½ cups chicken broth
1 cup apple cider
Pinch ground red pepper
½ cup heavy cream or half-and-half
Garnish: Cider Cream and thinly sliced scallions or chives

Bonnie's Tip:
Butternut squash is very hard, so I like to make a few slashes with a knife in the hard skin and microwave it on High for 3 to 5 minutes to soften it. Then place on a cutting board and split it vertically. Place cut side down on a rimmed baking sheet that is lined with parchment or foil for easy cleanup.

Roast in 375°F oven for 20 to 30 minutes until tender. Set aside until cool enough to handle. Scoop out seeds and membrane and discard. Scoop out pulp to use in the recipe and discard the rind.

1. Melt butter in heavy large saucepan over medium-high heat. Add onion, carrot and celery; sauté until slightly softened, about 5 minutes. Mix in squash, apple, thyme, sage and ginger.

2. Add broth and cider and bring to boil. Reduce heat to medium-low. Cover and simmer until vegetables and apple are tender, stirring occasionally, about 20 minutes. Cool slightly.

3. Working in batches, purée soup in blender or food processor, filling only half full. Leave feeder cap open for steam to escape and cover top with towel. Return soup to pan. Taste and add salt and ground red pepper as needed. Add cream.

4. Ladle into bowls. Drizzle with Cider Cream and sprinkle with scallions and serve. Makes 8 servings

Cider Cream
½ cup apple cider
⅔ cup sour cream

Boil cider in heavy small saucepan until reduced to 2 tablespoons, about 6 to 9 minutes. Cool. Whisk reduced cider into sour cream.

WILD RICE AND VEGETABLE PILAF

A lovely side dish brimming with wild rice, vegetable and herbs.

2 cups chicken broth
½ cup wild rice (not instant)
½ cup long-grain white rice (prefer Uncle
   Ben's converted – not instant)
2 tablespoons butter
1 garlic clove, minced
½ cup chopped onion

½ cup sliced fresh mushrooms
¼ teaspoon dried thyme leaves
Salt and pepper
1 cup fresh green beans, ends removed
   and cut into ½ inch pieces
1 cup diced carrots
1 tablespoons minced fresh parsley

1. **Combine** chicken broth and wild rice in medium saucepan; bring to a boil. Reduce heat, cover and simmer 30 minutes or until almost tender. Stir in white rice and bring back to a boil; reduce heat, cover and simmer for 20 minutes or until rices are tender.

2. **Meanwhile,** in a saucepan, melt butter over low heat; add garlic, onion, mushrooms and thyme. Season with salt and pepper. Sauté over medium-high heat for a few minutes or until softened and fragrant. Add carrots, green beans, and 1 cup water. Cover and cook until vegetables are tender, about 5 to 7 minutes. Drain liquid if any remains in the pan.

3. **Stir** vegetables into the rice; cook together until well heated. Taste and add salt and pepper as needed. Stir in parsley and serve. Makes 4 servings

MAPLE SMOKED CHICKEN

This is one of my favorite ways to enjoy chicken—it's smoky, tender and succulent. I use a stovetop smoker which makes it very easy to do. Once is in the smoker, I forget about it for nearly an hour, and then it is ready to serve it.

Dry Rub
1 teaspoon salt
1 teaspoon paprika
1 teaspoon garlic powder
½ teaspoon black pepper
¼ teaspoon ground red pepper, optional
½ teaspoon dried thyme
½ teaspoon dried oregano
2 tablespoons brown sugar

1 (3-pound) chicken, halved or meaty chicken parts (breasts, legs and thighs)
Maple wood chips for smoking

1. In a medium size bowl, mix together the ingredients for the dry rub. Rub the seasoning over surface of the chicken. Cover the chicken with plastic wrap and refrigerate 1 hour.

2. Place 3 tablespoons maple wood chips in the center of the smoker. Line the drip tray with foil for easy clean up. Spray the rack with nonstick spray if desired (makes cleanup easier). Place the chicken on the rack. Slide lid on the pan but leave an inch or so open. Place smoker over medium heat. When you see smoke coming out of the pan, close the lid completely. Smoke the chicken for 40 to 50 minutes or until the chicken registers 165°F. Makes 4 servings

Bonnie's Tip:
A stovetop smoker can be used on a gas range, electric range with coil or the grill. It is an easy and efficient way to infuse that deep, slow-smoked flavor into meat, poultry and fish. Stovetop smokers can be purchased at specialty cookware stores.

CRANBERRY APRICOT CHUTNEY

This beautiful chutney keeps well in the refrigerator and is excellent with pork as well as poultry.

1 cup cranberry juice
1 ½ cups fresh or frozen cranberries
⅔ cup dried apricots, coarsely chopped
⅔ cup sugar
¼ teaspoon salt
¼ teaspoon red pepper flakes
½ cup chopped walnuts, lightly toasted

Combine all ingredients, except walnuts, together in a heavy saucepan. Bring to a boil and simmer until thickened to a syrup consistency, about 10 minutes. Stir in chopped walnuts. Serve warm or at room temperature. Makes about 2 ¾ cups

HOT LEMON SOUFFLÉ WITH RASPBERRY SAUCE

This is perfection! It's light, lofty and brimming with the fresh taste of lemon.

2 tablespoons butter, melted, for soufflé
   dishes
¼ cup sugar for soufflé dishes
¼ cup (½ stick) butter, melted
⅓ cup all-purpose flour
1 ⅓ cups milk

⅔ cup sugar, divided use
1 ½ tablespoons lemon zest
⅓ cup fresh-squeezed lemon juice
5 large eggs, separated
Powdered sugar

1. Preheat the oven to 350°F. Brush inside of eight 4-ounce-individual-soufflé dishes (or a 7-cup soufflé dish) well with melted butter. Put the sugar inside one dish and toss to coat, then tip the excess sugar into the next dish and repeat.

2. Melt butter in a small saucepan over medium heat. Stir in flour and cook and stir for a minute. Whisk in milk, ⅓ cup sugar and lemon zest, and cook over medium heat until mixture boils and thickens, stirring constantly. Stir in lemon juice. Set aside and let cool for 15 minutes. Whisk egg yolks and stir into the milk mixture.

3. In a mixer fitted with a whisk attachment, whip the egg whites in a clean dry bowl until soft peaks form. Gradually add the remaining sugar and continue whipping until stiff and glossy. Fold whites into the milk mixture.

4. Divide mixture among prepared soufflé dishes, filling them three-quarters full. Run your thumb around the inside rim of each dish, making a shallow "moat" around the edge of the batter. This encourages the soufflés to rise straight up. Sift powdered sugar over the surface of the soufflés. (The uncooked soufflés can stand at this point for up to 30 minutes in the refrigerator.)

5. Bake soufflés in the center of the oven 20 to 25 minutes until puffed and light golden brown. Serve the hot soufflés with raspberry sauce. Make a small opening in each soufflé with a fork and drizzle raspberry sauce over the top. Makes about 8 individual (4-ounce) servings

Raspberry Sauce
1 (12-ounce) bag frozen unsweetened raspberries, thawed
½ cup sugar
1 teaspoon lemon juice

Simmer berries, sugar and lemon juice in small saucepan over medium heat for 4 to 5 minutes or until berries have released their juice and broken apart. Strain to remove seeds. Serve warm with soufflés.

VINEYARD
Feast

I enjoy visiting vineyards, particularly the older ones shrouded with rich histories and located in picturesque areas. The whole process fascinates me: the planting and nurturing of the vines, the labor that goes into creating acres where fruit hangs heavy on the vine, and ultimately, the harvest. After the harvest, comes the feast!

When the grape harvest is complete, it is time to celebrate with fabulous food. The spiced pistachios used in the salad are quite

addictive — you may want to make an extra batch. The blackberry reduction pairs beautifully with the roasted loin of pork. But the dessert here is a show-stopper. It boasts a hazelnut crust, a creamy filling flavored with white chocolate and Frangelico, and garnished with fresh raspberries.

VINEYARD FEAST

Spinach Salad with Gorgonzola,
Spiced Pistachios and Warm Sherry
Vinaigrette

Roasted Loin of Pork with
Blackberry Reduction

Wild Rice Pilaf with Cranberries
and Almonds

Cauliflower Broccoli Gratin
with Walnuts

Hazelnut White Chocolate Cheesecake

SPINACH SALAD WITH GORGONZOLA, SPICED PISTACHIOS AND WARM SHERRY VINAIGRETTE

A simple but delicious salad. The sweet spiced pistachios and the sharp notes of the Gorgonzola are a very complementary taste combination.

12 cups fresh baby spinach, washed and spun dry
½ cup raspberries, optional
4 to 6 ounces Gorgonzola cheese, broken into chunks
1 cup warm Sherry Vinaigrette (recipe follows)
½ cup Spiced Pistachios (recipe follows)

1. Place spinach on 8 salad plates. Top with pieces of Gorgonzola cheese and berries.

2. Heat 1 cup Sherry Vinaigrette in a small saucepan or glass measure in the microwave until hot but not boiling. Pour warm dressing over the salads; sprinkle with a few spiced pistachios and serve immediately. Makes 8 servings

Sherry Vinaigrette
⅓ cup sherry vinegar
2 garlic cloves, minced
½ small onion, chopped
¾ teaspoon salt
¼ teaspoon ground black pepper
1 ½ cups olive oil
2 tablespoons chopped parsley

Combine vinegar, garlic, onion, salt and pepper in a blender. Process until blended. Slowly drizzle in oil through small opening in blender lid until dressing thickens and is emulsified. Stir in chopped parsley. Makes about 1 ¾ cups

Spiced Pistachios
¼ cup sugar
2 tablespoons water
1 teaspoon cinnamon
1 ground red pepper
¼ teaspoon rosemary
2 cups salted pistachios

1. Preheat oven to 350°F. Spray a cookie sheet with nonstick vegetable spray or line with parchment. In small saucepan over medium heat, cook sugar and water until sugar is dissolved. Stir in cinnamon, red pepper and rosemary. Add pistachios and stir to coat with sugar mixture.

2. Place nuts in a single layer in pan and roast for 7 to 9 minutes in oven. Cool. Store in covered container. They are good "keepers", as long as you stay out of them!

WILD RICE WITH DRIED CRANBERRIES AND ALMONDS

This wild rice dish has outstanding flavors and textures and goes nicely with both pork and poultry.

⅓ cup butter
1 large onion, chopped
1 garlic clove, minced
3 ½ cups canned low-salt chicken broth
1 cup (about 6 ounces) wild rice
1 cup long-grain rice (prefer Uncle Ben's Converted Rice)
1 teaspoon dried leaf thyme
½ teaspoon salt
¼ to ½ teaspoon freshly ground black pepper
1 cup dried cranberries
½ cup thinly sliced green onions (including green tops)
⅓ cup chopped fresh parsley
½ cup slivered almonds, toasted

1. Melt butter in heavy pan over medium-high heat. Add onions and garlic and sauté until tender, about 4 minutes. Add chicken broth, bring to boil and then add wild rice. Reduce heat to medium-low. Cover and simmer 40 minutes.

2. Add long-grain rice, thyme, salt and pepper. Cover and simmer until rice is just tender and most liquid is absorbed, about 20 minutes longer.

3. Stir in cranberries; cover and cook until liquid is absorbed, about 5 minutes longer. Add onions, parsley and toasted almonds. Makes 8 to 10 servings

CAULIFLOWER BROCCOLI GRATIN WITH WALNUTS

No doubt this is the ultimate cauliflower broccoli casserole. The sauce and crumb top escalates this vegetable dish to a whole new level.

2 pounds broccoli, broken into florets
2 pounds cauliflower, broken into florets

Sauce
½ cup butter
½ cup flour
¾ teaspoon salt
⅛ teaspoon ground red pepper
4 cups milk
8 ounces grated sharp Cheddar cheese

Crumb Topping
2 cups fresh breadcrumbs
¼ cup butter
1 cup coarsely chopped walnuts

1. Heat 3 quarts of water and 2 teaspoons salt in a large pot until it comes to a boil. Add broccoli and cauliflower. Cook until tender-crisp, about 3 to 4 minutes. Drain. Refresh with cold water; drain and set aside.

2. Heat butter in a heavy saucepan over medium heat. Add flour, salt and ground red pepper. Cook for a minute or two, then whisk in milk. Cook, stirring constantly, until mixture comes to a boil and thickens. Add cheese; stir until melted. Set aside.

3. Combine breadcrumbs, butter and walnuts.

4. Place vegetables in large, shallow, buttered casserole dish. Spoon sauce over vegetables. Top with crumb mixture. (May be covered and refrigerated at this point.) Bake in preheated 350°F oven for 30 minutes until hot and bubbly. Makes 12 servings

ROASTED LOIN OF PORK WITH BLACKBERRY REDUCTION

Pork is a very lean cut and benefits from the time in the brine. This one needs to set overnight in the refrigerator and will be ready to finish the next day. You will find it tender, juicy and with great flavor.

Brine
1 quart water
½ cup salt
½ cup sugar
2 bay leaves
1 teaspoon dried thyme
1 tablespoon whole black peppercorns

1 (3-pound) center-cut boneless pork loin
1 tablespoon olive oil
1 garlic clove, minced
½ teaspoon dried rosemary
Salt and pepper

Blackberry Sauce
1 ½ cups (about 8 ounces) frozen
    unsweetened blackberries, thawed,
    pureed and strained
3 tablespoons butter, divided use
½ cup minced onion
⅓ cup dry white wine
1 cup chicken stock
2 teaspoons fresh lemon juice
¼ cup seedless blackberry jam
¼ teaspoon ground black pepper
¼ teaspoon salt (or more to taste)
Garnish: Fresh rosemary

1. For the Brine: In a large pot, bring the water to a boil. Add salt, sugar, bay leaves, thyme and peppercorns. Simmer for 5 minutes. Cool down with ice; adding enough ice to totally cool the brine. Pour the brine into a large container; add the pork. Cover and refrigerate overnight.

2. For the Roasted Pork Loin: Remove the pork loin from the brine. Pat dry.

3. Preheat oven to 350°F. Combine olive oil, minced garlic and rosemary in a small dish. Rub over surface of the roast. Season to taste with salt and pepper. Place on a rack in a roasting pan and roast 45 to 60 minutes or until the internal temperature reaches 155°F. Remove from oven. Transfer roast from the pan to a cutting board, tent with foil and let rest at least 15 minutes. Set roasting pan aside for later use.

4. For the Sauce: Put blackberries in food processor or blender and puree. Run through mesh strainer to remove seeds. Set aside.

5. Place roasting pan over medium heat. Add 1 tablespoon butter and onion; sauté onion until tender, stirring occasionally. Deglaze pan with wine and chicken stock; bring to a boil and reduce by half, scraping up the browned bits. Stir in lemon juice, blackberry puree, jam, salt and pepper to taste. Turn off heat. Whisk in remaining butter. Serve sauce with sliced pork loin and garnish with rosemary. Makes 8 servings

HAZELNUT WHITE CHOCOLATE CHEESECAKE

Crust
¾ cup hazelnuts
1 cup graham cracker crumbs
¼ cup sugar
⅓ cup butter, melted

Filling
6 ounces white chocolate, chopped in
　small pieces
4 (8-ounce) packages cream cheese,
　room temperature
1 cup sugar
2 tablespoons hazelnut liqueur
　(Frangelico), optional
2 teaspoons vanilla extract
4 large eggs

Raspberry Coulis
1 (12-ounce) bag frozen raspberries,
　thawed
⅓ cup sugar

Garnish: Whipped cream, fresh
　raspberries, powdered sugar (optional)

1. For the Crust: Preheat oven to 350°F. Place hazelnuts in pie pan and roast until brown, about 15 minutes, and most of the skins are split. Roll hot hazelnuts in a towel and set aside to steam for 10 minutes. Rub hazelnuts with a towel to remove husks. Cool. Place in a zipper top plastic bag and crush coarsely with a rolling pin.

2. Combine hazelnuts, graham cracker crumbs, sugar and butter. Butter bottom and sides of a 9-inch spring form pan. Press crumbs firmly into bottom of pan, packing down tightly. Bake 10 minutes. Cool. Wrap outside of pan in double layer of heavy-duty aluminum wrap to prevent leaking while cheesecake bakes in a hot water bath. Foil should come all the way to the top of the pan and be pressed snuggly against pan to prevent leakage

3. To prepare the Filling: Place white chocolate in microwave-safe container; microwave for 1 minute; remove and stir. If necessary, microwave for additional 10 second intervals until just melted—watch it, chocolate will burn easily! Set aside.

4. Beat cream cheese with electric mixer on high speed until light and creamy. Add sugar, liqueur and vanilla; beat 2 minutes or until sugar is dissolved. With mixer running, add melted white chocolate; beat until combined. Reduce speed to low and add eggs, one at a time, beating just until combined.

5. Pour batter into prepared crust. Set the cheesecake in a larger pan (i.e. roasting pan); place in preheated 350°F oven. Carefully pour hot water into larger pan until water comes half-way up the side of the cheesecake. Bake for 45 minutes. Turn off oven without opening door; leave cheesecake in oven for 1 hour. Transfer cake to rack and cool to room temperature. Cover with plastic wrap and chill overnight. Serve with raspberry coulis, whipped cream and fresh raspberrires. Dust with powdered sugar before serving if desired.

6. For the Raspberry Coulis: Puree raspberries with sugar in blender or food processor. Strain to remove seeds. Serve sauce with cheesecake. Makes one 9-inch cheesecake

Northern
ITALIAN
DINNER

From the regions of Northern Italy comes a more refined cooking style. The rich, fertile land sustains cattle production; consequently, butter and other dairy products are used extensively in the north. One will find more stuffed pastas made with dairy-based sauces rather than tomato sauces that are favored in southern Italy.

I have taught this menu probably a dozen times over the years and it is timeless — each class thinks it is the best! Also, I enjoy making the cannelloni for guests because everyone loves it and it can be prepared a day in advance. I will never forget the first time I made the focaccia; I was testing the recipe for an upcoming class. It smelled and looked beautiful; I cut a small sliver and tasted it. It was really good! I found I kept going back to the kitchen for just another small taste. Soon, a good portion of it had disappeared and I had to put it away to keep from nibbling.

NORTHERN ITALIAN DINNER

Pasta Fagiola

Rosemary Focaccia

Romaine, Tomato and Artichoke Salad

Northern Italian Chicken Cannelloni
with Two Sauces

Lemon Swirl Cheesecake

PASTA FAGIOLA

A rich, satisfying classic soup that is loaded with vegetables, beans and pasta, then liberally seasoned with herbs. Good warmed over if there is any left.

1 to 2 tablespoons olive oil
1 small onion, finely chopped (about ½ cup)
1 medium carrot, peeled and shredded
½ medium green pepper, finely chopped
2 cloves garlic, minced
3 cups beef broth
⅓ cup tomato juice
¼ cup dry red wine
1 bay leaf
½ teaspoon dried basil

½ teaspoon dried leaf oregano
Pinch crushed red pepper
¼ teaspoon freshly ground black pepper
½ cup dried small tubular or shell pasta
1 small zucchini, chopped
1 (16-ounce) can small red beans, rinsed and drained
1 (16-ounce) can cannellini beans, rinsed and drained
Garnish: Minced fresh parsley

Bonnie's Tip:
Cannellini beans are frequently found in the canned bean section of supermarkets. They are a large, white bean. Great Northern beans may be substituted if cannellinis are not available.

1. Heat olive oil in skillet or Dutch oven. Add onions, carrot, green pepper and garlic. Cover and cook until vegetables are tender, about 3 to 4 minutes.

2. Add beef broth, tomato juice, wine and all the seasonings. Bring to a boil. Add pasta and zucchini to the boiling broth mixture. Cook until pasta is tender, about 10 minutes, stirring frequently.

3. Meanwhile, remove one-half cup of the broth from the soup and place in blender or food processor along with one-half of the rinsed and drained red beans. Process until blended. Add pureed mixture to the soup to thicken it.

4. Add remaining red beans and white beans to the soup. Heat until soup comes to a simmer, stirring occasionally. Garnish with fresh parsley and serve. Makes about 1 quart

ROMAINE, TOMATO AND ARTICHOKE SALAD

Bits of artichoke in the salad dressing add a delightful element of surprise to this salad.

¼ cup red wine vinegar
1 garlic clove
1 tablespoon fresh lemon juice
1 tablespoon Dijon mustard
1 tablespoon honey
¼ teaspoon salt
⅛ teaspoon crushed red pepper
½ cup extra virgin olive oil
5 tablespoons mayonnaise (prefer Hellmann's)
1 (15-ounce) can artichoke hearts, rinsed and drained
12 cups washed, dried and torn romaine and endive leaves
½ small red onion, thinly sliced
2 medium tomatoes, cut into wedges
Garnish: Freshly shredded Parmesan cheese

1. For the Dressing: Combine vinegar, garlic, lemon juice, mustard, honey, salt and pepper in a food processor or blender. Process until mixed. Gradually add olive oil. Add mayonnaise and pulse a few times until blended. Add about one-third of the drained artichokes and pulse machine on-and-off until chopped. Transfer to a covered container and chill. (Dressing will keep well for 3 days.)

2. For the Salad: Combine romaine, red onion and tomatoes in a bowl. Toss with enough dressing to coat. Divide salad among plates. Top with remaining artichokes and Parmesan cheese. Makes 6 to 8 servings

NORTHERN ITALIAN CHICKEN CANNELLONI WITH TWO SAUCES

Don't let the long ingredient list discourage you. Each part may be done in stages. I have served this many times to groups and it is the ideal entrée because it can be assembled in advance and refrigerated for a day or two. Leftovers freeze beautifully.

Chicken Filling
2 tablespoons olive oil
2 cloves garlic, minced
½ large onion, chopped
½ cup chopped red bell pepper
½ cup chopped celery
1 (15-ounce) carton ricotta cheese
1 egg, slightly beaten
2 cups (8 ounces) shredded Monterey Jack cheese
½ cup thinly sliced green onions (green parts included)
½ cup grated Parmesan cheese
2 teaspoons dried basil (or 2 to 3 tablespoons fresh chopped basil)
½ teaspoon dried oregano
¾ to 1 teaspoon salt
¼ teaspoon ground red pepper
1 pound cooked chicken breast, coarsely chopped

12 to 16 manicotti cannelloni, cooked and drained

Parmesan Sauce
6 tablespoons butter
6 tablespoons flour
2 ¼ cups milk
1 ½ cup chicken broth
½ teaspoon salt
¼ teaspoon ground red pepper
½ cup grated Parmesan cheese

Topping
3 cups shredded Mozzarella cheese
Garnish: ½ cup pesto sauce or Ragu sauce, commercial or homemade

Bonnie's Tip:
Cooked manicotti cannelloni are much easier to fill if you split them open, lay them flat, then wrap back into a cylinder shape and place them seam-side down in the pan. When baked, no one can tell they had been split.

1. For the Chicken Filling: Heat olive oil in a sauté pan over medium heat. Add garlic, onion, red bell pepper and celery. Sauté until tender, 2 to 4 minutes. Combine sautéed vegetables with all remaining chicken filling ingredients, mix completely.

2. To make the Parmesan Sauce: Melt butter in heavy saucepan. Stir in flour, cook until bubbly. Add milk, chicken broth, salt and red pepper. Cook, stirring constantly, until sauce boils and is thickened. Remove pan from heat. Stir Parmesan cheese into sauce.

3. To assemble the Cannelloni: Preheat oven to 375°F. Cannelloni may be baked in two 9x13-inch baking pans or baked in individual au gratin dishes. Either way, oil the pan or spray with cooking spray. Spread a thin layer of Parmesan sauce on the bottom of pans.

4. Split each cooked pasta tube so it will lie flat. Spoon about ⅓ cup chicken filling in a cylinder along center of the pasta. Roll to enclose. Place seam-side down in prepared pan. Repeat until all cannelloni are filled.

5. Pour remaining Parmesan Sauce over cannelloni. Be sure to cover all parts of the pasta to keep it moist while baking. Sprinkle mozzarella over the top. Bake in a preheated 375°F oven for 30 minutes or until bubbly and golden.

6. To serve: Place 1 or 2 cannelloni on plate, and garnish with a zigzag of Pesto Sauce or Ragu sauce from a squeeze bottle. Makes 8 servings (2 each) or 16 servings (1 each)

This recipe makes a large quantity. Extras may be wrapped well and frozen for later enjoyment.

ROSEMARY FOCACCIA

I will never forget the first time I tested this recipe several years ago. After it was baked, I cut off a piece to sample—it was so good I didn't want to stop sampling . . . and much of it disappeared very quickly that afternoon.

1 package (or 1 tablespoon) dry yeast
1 cup warm water (105 to 115°F)
3 ¼ to 3 ½ cups unbleached or all-purpose flour
1 ⅓ cups mashed potatoes
2 tablespoons extra virgin olive oil, plus more for oiling pans
1 ½ teaspoons salt

Topping
3 tablespoons olive oil
2 cloves minced garlic
2 tablespoons minced fresh rosemary (or 2 teaspoons dried rosemary, crumbled)
1 teaspoon coarsely ground black pepper
Kosher salt to taste

FOOD PROCESSOR METHOD:

1. In work bowl of food processor fitted with the metal blade, pulse yeast, ½ cup flour and ½ cup warm water until combined. Put the lid on the work bowl and let stand for 20 minutes or until bubbly. Add 2 ¾ cups flour, rest of the water, potatoes, oil and salt. Process until the dough is smooth and elastic. If too soft, add enough flour so dough will form around middle of the bowl, but it should be a soft, pliable dough.

OR HAND METHOD:

1. In a large bowl, combine yeast, flour and water. Let stand until foamy, about 20 minutes. Add remaining ingredients as stated above. Turn mixture onto a lightly floured board; knead until dough is springy and elastic, 8 to 10 minutes.

THEN FOR EITHER METHOD:

2. Turn dough out onto a work surface that is lightly floured. Cut in half. Oil two 10-inch pizza pans with olive oil. Form each piece of dough into a flat disc about 10 inches in diameter. Cover dough with lightly greased or oil-sprayed plastic wrap. Let rise 30 minutes. Remove plastic wrap and make dimples with oiled or wet fingers.

3. Mix oil and garlic and drizzle it over the dough. Sprinkle with rosemary, black pepper and salt. Preheat oven to 425°F and adjust rack to lower one-third of oven. Bake focaccia until golden and crisp, about 20 to 25 minutes. Transfer to wire rack to cool slightly. Cut into wedges and serve warm or room temperature.

Makes two 10-inch-focaccia breads

Bonnie's Tip:
Baked focaccia may be kept on a counter for several hours and reheated before serving. Or wrap cooled focaccia well and freeze up to 1 month. Unwrap and warm in 350°F oven for about 15 minutes.

The secret to the wonderful texture of this bread is the mashed potatoes. Yeast feed upon the starch in the potato and works pure magic. It is fine to use instant mashed potatoes, but be sure you reconstitute them according to the package directions.

LEMON SWIRL CHEESECAKE

Lemon curd and cheesecake—this is a lovely cheesecake with a terrific marriage of flavors.

Lemon curd
3 large eggs
1 teaspoon finely grated fresh lemon zest
½ cup fresh lemon juice
½ cup sugar
½ stick (¼ cup) butter, cut into small pieces

Crust
1 ⅔ cup finely ground graham cracker crumbs
⅓ cup sugar
¼ teaspoon salt
5 tablespoons butter, melted

Filling
3 (8-ounce) packages cream cheese, room temperature
1 cup sugar
3 large eggs
¾ cup sour cream
1 teaspoon vanilla
Garnish: Whipped cream and lemon zest

1. For the Lemon Curd: Place eggs in a 2-cup measure and whisk well. Pour into a 2-quart heavy saucepan with zest, juice, sugar, and butter. Cook over moderately low heat, stirring constantly, until mixture thickens and it begins to boil. Remove from heat. Strain into a bowl using a spatula to scrape the bottom of the sieve. Cover top with plastic; cool.

2. For the Crust: Preheat oven to 350°F. Combine crust ingredients in a bowl, mixing well. Butter the bottom of a 9-inch springform pan. Press crumb mixture into the bottom of the pan, but not the sides. Bake 10 minutes to set the crust. Cool. Wrap outside of pan in double layer of heavy-duty aluminum wrap to prevent leaking while cheesecake bakes in a hot water bath.

3. For the Filling: Beat together cream cheese and sugar in a bowl with an electric mixer at medium speed until smooth, 1 to 2 minutes. Reduce speed to low and add eggs 1 at a time, beating until incorporated. Beat in sour cream and vanilla until combined.

4. Pour two-thirds of cream cheese filling into crust, then drop half of lemon curd over filling in spoonfuls, and swirl curd into filling with a small knife to make a marble effect. Repeat with remaining filling and curd.

5. Set the cheesecake in a larger pan (i.e. roasting pan); place in preheated 350°F oven. Carefully pour hot water into larger pan until water comes halfway up the side of the cheesecake. Bake for 1 hour. Turn off oven without opening door; leave cheesecake in oven for another hour. Transfer cake to rack; remove foil carefully and allow to cool at room temperature for an hour. Cover with plastic wrap and chill overnight.

6. Before serving, garnish if desired with whipped cream and lemon zest.

Makes 12 servings

Showstopper
DINNER

When nothing but the best will do, it is time to pull out the Showstopper Dinner. It is rich, decadent and actually makes any celebration noteworthy. It has all the things we love — crisp salad with a warm Brie dressing, beef tenderloin with a fabulous but easy sauce, interesting side dishes and a beautifully presented dessert.

The salad is truly unusual, warm brie dressing ladled over fresh greens, juicy pears and toasted walnuts. If you have never had beef tenderloin with a blue-veined cheese sauce, you will be in for a pleasant surprise. The flavors marry beautifully and create a fabulous entrée. But the heavenly crescent rolls may very well be the stars of the menu — I have been making these for years and they are one of my signature recipes.

SHOWSTOPPER DINNER

Mixed Greens with Warm Brie Fondue
and Winter Pear Slices

Herb Roasted Beef Tenderloin with
Mushroom Gorgonzola Sauce

Potato Soufflé Gratinee

Green Bean Carrot Bundles
with Bacon

Heavenly Crescent Rolls

White Chocolate Raspberry Tiramisu
with Chocolate Leaves

MIXED GREENS WITH WARM BRIE FONDUE AND WINTER PEAR SLICES

A simple but elegant salad that will make any occasion special!

Brie Fondue Dressing
2 tablespoons olive oil
1 small shallot, minced
1 ⅓ cup heavy cream
12 ounces brie, rind trimmed and cut into 1 inch pieces
1 teaspoon Dijon mustard
2 tablespoons sherry vinegar
½ teaspoon salt
⅛ to ¼ teaspoon ground red pepper

16 cups assorted torn greens (Boston lettuce, romaine and/or mixed baby greens)
¾ cup walnuts, toasted and coarsely chopped
3 ripe but firm pears, cored and thinly sliced

1. For the Dressing: Heat oil in a 2 quart saucepan over medium low heat. Add shallot and sauté until softened, about 2 minutes. Add cream and bring to a simmer. Remove from heat and stir in brie, stirring until cheese is melted. If necessary, place pan back over very low heat just until cheese is melted, stirring constantly and mixture is creamy.

2. When cheese is melted, stir in mustard, vinegar, salt and ground red pepper.

3. To assemble salad: Arrange greens on salad plates. Top with walnuts and pears. Pass warm Brie Dressing. Makes 8 servings

Bonnie's Tip:
If the mixture separates in the first step and does not become smooth, put it in blender and give it a whirl to smooth out. You may need to add a little milk if it is too thick. (Be sure to leave a small opening on the blender and place a clean towel over the opening; never seal tightly and blend a hot liquid. It may "explode").

GREEN BEAN CARROT BUNDLES WITH BACON

A beautiful do-ahead treatment for vegetables and they are pretty on the plate, too!

2 pounds fresh green beans, ends removed
2 medium carrots, cut into strips about the same size as green beans
8 thin bacon slices, precooked but not crisp
⅓ cup butter, melted
¼ cup light brown sugar
Salt and pepper
Garnish: finely chopped red bell pepper (optional)

1. Blanche green beans and carrots in boiling salted water for 2 to 3 minutes or until tender-crisp. Drain. Immerse in cold water to stop cooking and to set the color.

2. Gather 8 to 12 green beans and 3 carrot strips in bundles and wrap a piece of bacon around center of each bundle. Place bundles on baking pan with bacon ends facing down on the pan. (Recipe may be prepared to this stage, pan covered tightly and chilled until ready for serving.)

3. Lavishly brush or drizzle butter over vegetables. Sprinkle with brown sugar; season generously with salt and pepper. Drizzle with melted butter. Bake 15 minutes or until bacon is browned and crisp. If desired, garnish each with a sprinkling of red bell pepper. Makes 8 servings

HERB ROASTED BEEF TENDERLOIN WITH MUSHROOM GORGONZOLA SAUCE

A terrific blending of flavors—the rich taste of beef accented with the sharp bite of the Gorgonzola.

2 tablespoons olive oil
3 garlic cloves, minced
1 (4 to 5-pound) beef tenderloin, well trimmed
1 teaspoon salt
1 teaspoon freshly ground black pepper

1 teaspoon dried leaf basil
½ teaspoon dried leaf thyme
¼ teaspoon dried rosemary
1 cup dry red wine, divided use
Garnish: Fresh herbs (optional)

1. Preheat oven to 375°F. Combine oil with garlic. Rub the tenderloin surface with oil-garlic mixture. Season with salt and pepper.

2. Combine basil, thyme and rosemary. Sprinkle over surface of meat.

3. Fold under small end of tenderloin for uniform shape so meat will roast evenly. Tie with cotton string at 1 ½ inch intervals for more uniform cooking.

4. Place tenderloin on rack in roasting pan. Pour ½ cup wine in roasting pan. Roast uncovered in preheated oven for 40 to 60 minutes or until meat thermometer registers 135°F for medium rare, basting occasionally with remaining wine.

5. Remove to platter; tent with foil to keep warm. Let stand 15 to 20 minutes for juices to stabilize before carving. Serve with Mushroom Gorgonzola Sauce.

Mushroom Gorgonzola Sauce
½ cup butter
½ pound mushrooms, sliced
½ cup chopped green onions (tops included)
2 cloves garlic
4 ounces Gorgonzola cheese (or other blue-veined cheese)
1 tablespoon Worcestershire sauce

1. In a medium skillet over low heat, melt butter. Add mushrooms, green onions and garlic. Cook, stirring frequently until moisture evaporates and mushrooms are soft. Add cheese and Worcestershire sauce.

2. Cook and stir until cheese is melted and hot. Serve immediately with tenderloin.
Makes 8 to 10 servings

Bonnie's Tip:
Gorgonzola is a blue-veined cheese that is thought to have originated in the Middle Ages in the small town of Gorgonzola, near Milan. I typically use it to top salads or pizza, or melt it into risotto or various pasta dishes. One of my favorite ways to use Gorgonzola is to make a creamy, flavorful sauce to enhance beef tenderloin.

POTATOES SOUFFLÉ GRATINÉE

This dish is beautiful for two reasons – it tastes great, but it can also be made ahead, covered and chilled. If chilled, it will need to bake for 1 to 1 ¼ hours, or until puffed and golden.

3 pounds baking potatoes, peeled
2 teaspoons salt, divided use
1 (8-ounce) package cream cheese
3 large eggs
½ to ¾ cup cream or half-and-half
1 head roasted garlic pulp, optional (see margin note)
1 teaspoon salt

1/8 teaspoon ground red pepper
½ cup thinly sliced green onions
1 cup fresh bread crumbs
2 tablespoons grated Parmesan cheese
1 tablespoon fresh parsley, minced
1 tablespoon butter, melted (plus additional for buttering casserole)

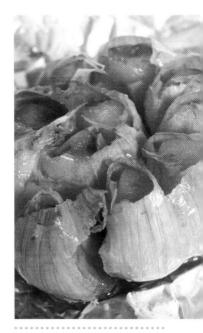

1. Butter an 8-cup soufflé dish or 8 individual ramekins. Set aside. Preheat oven to 350°F.

2. Peel potatoes; cut into quarters. Place potatoes in a large saucepan over high heat with 1 teaspoon salt and enough water to cover; bring to a boil. Reduce heat to low; cover and simmer 20 to 30 minutes or until potatoes are tender. Drain well.

3. While still hot, mash potatoes with cream cheese, eggs and ½ cup cream, adding additional cream if needed. Squeeze roasted garlic pulp into potatoes. Season with remaining teaspoon salt and ground red pepper. Fold in green onions. Pour into buttered soufflé dish or ramekins, leaving 2 inches at the top for expansion.

4. Combine bread crumbs, Parmesan, parsley and butter. Sprinkle over top. Bake at 350°F for 45 minutes. Makes 8 servings

For Roasted Garlic: Remove the outer white papery skin from the garlic head. Do not separate cloves or peel garlic. Cut a thin slice off the top just to expose the garlic clove. Place each head on a square of aluminum foil. Drizzle a teaspoon of olive oil on the cut surface. Wrap securely in aluminum foil. Bake at 350°F for 1 hour. Cool 10 minutes. Separate cloves and squeeze to extract pulp.

Herb Roasted Beef Tenderloin with Mushroom Gargonzola Sauce, p.178

WHITE CHOCOLATE RASPBERRY TIRAMISU WITH CHOCOLATE LEAVES

These individual tiramisu look super-elegant served in stemmed wine glasses. Make the tiramisu a day ahead, but wait to top with raspberries at serving time.

White Chocolate Cream
4 ounces white chocolate, chopped into small pieces
½ cup milk
8 ounces cream cheese or mascarpone, room temperature
¼ cup sugar
¾ cup heavy cream
1 teaspoon vanilla extract

16 very thin slices sponge or angel food cake
¼ cup raspberry-flavored syrup or Chambord liqueur
⅓ cup finely grated semisweet chocolate
Garnish: Fresh raspberries, whipped cream, chocolate leaves

Bonnie's Tip:
Mascarpone is a mild, triple-cream cheese prevalent in Italy and is less tart than cream cheese. Sometimes, it is difficult to find in certain areas. If unavailable, substitute cream cheese—it works very well in this recipe.

1. Place the white chocolate pieces in a small bowl. Heat milk in a microwave-safe glass measure for 30 to 45 seconds or until very hot but not boiling. (Exact time depends upon the power of your microwave). Pour the hot milk over chocolate. Whisk until the chocolate is completely melted. Cool to room temperature.

2. Meanwhile, in a medium bowl, beat mascarpone cheese until soft and light. Add sugar and beat until creamy. Fold the cooled white chocolate mixture into the cream cheese mixture. Set aside.

3. In a small, chilled bowl, whip the cream with the vanilla until soft peaks form. Do not overbeat.

4. Fold the whipped cream into the white chocolate-cream cheese mixture. The texture should be like lightly whipped cream; if it doesn't "flow", thin the mixture slightly by stirring in milk, 1 tablespoon at a time.

5. Place a small piece of the cake into the bottom of eight wine glasses. Drizzle each with a couple of teaspoons of raspberry syrup. Spoon half of the cream mixture over the cake slices (about 2 ½ tablespoons for each slice.) Sprinkle each with ½ tablespoon of the grated chocolate. Repeat the layering: cake, cream mixture and chocolate layers. Cover and refrigerate for 8 to 48 hours.

6. Before serving, top each tiramisu with a pouf of whipped cream, a raspberry and a chocolate leaf.

Chocolate Leaves
½ cup grated semisweet chocolate
8 firm, fresh rose or lemon leaves, washed (be sure any leaf you use is non-poisonous!)

1. **Line** a plate with waxed paper or parchment. Place chocolate in a microwave-safe glass measure, and microwave on High for 15 seconds; stir and then microwave in 5 second increments until soft enough to melt when stirred. (Remember chocolate does not appear melted, you must stir it to check the consistency!).

2. **Using** a small brush or knife spread the underside of each leaf with a layer of chocolate. Be sure not to seal the edges with melted chocolate. Place the painted leaves, chocolate side up, on the prepared plate. Chill until the chocolate is set. Carefully peel the leaf off the chocolate, handling the chocolate leaf as little as possible. Return the leaves to the freezer if the chocolate is melting. Makes 8 servings

HEAVENLY CRESCENT ROLLS

These rolls are light as a feather with a wonderfully rich flavor. I've made this recipe for years. For holiday gatherings, I am often requested to bring "The Rolls"—which happens to be this recipe.

1 package active dry yeast	1 teaspoon salt
1 cup warm milk (100 to 110°F)	3 eggs
1 teaspoon sugar	4 to 4 ½ cups flour
½ cup shortening	Melted butter
½ cup sugar	

1. **Dissolve** yeast in warm milk with 1 teaspoon sugar; set aside for five minutes or until mixture becomes foamy. (Using a thermometer is a fool-proof way to determine the temperature of the liquid for dissolving the yeast. You want luke-warm liquid, not too hot or it will kill the yeast. If too cool, yeast will be slow to activate and to rise.) Beat shortening, sugar and salt in electric mixer at low speed. Add milk and yeast mixture to it. Beat on low to mix.

2. **Add** eggs and beat until well mixed. Stir in 2 cups flour and beat at medium speed for 2 minutes to develop the gluten.

3. **Stir** in enough remaining flour to make soft dough. Turn dough on floured board and knead only a few times until smooth. Place in a greased bowl and let rise until doubled in bulk (about 1 ½ hours).

4. **Turn** dough out (without working too much) on a floured board. Divide dough in half. Roll each half on a lightly floured surface to a 12-inch circle.

5. **Brush** with melted butter and cut each circle into 12 wedges. Roll up each wedge beginning at the wide end. Arrange rolls, point down, on greased baking sheet at least 2 ½ inches apart. Repeat with other half. Cover loosely with plastic wrap or damp towel. Let rise until very light and doubled in size.

6. **Bake** on middle rack in preheated 350°F oven for 10 to 12 minutes or until just pale golden. Serve immediately. Makes 24 rolls

Bonnie's Tip:
After rolls are shaped, they may be placed on a baking sheet and frozen. Once frozen, store in a zip-lock bag. To use: Remove from bag and place on a lightly greased baking sheet, 2 inches apart, as they will rise a great deal. Cover loosely with plastic wrap and let rise in a warm place for 5 hours. Bake as directed above. (For full rising power, store in freezer no longer than 10 days.)

DOWN HOME
Comfort

The first time I demonstrated how to make Kentucky Hot Browns in a cooking class, the students raved for weeks. They declared it was the ultimate "comfort food." This menu is a great brunch, lunch or supper — actually good any time you want to make it.

One of the ideal times to make this menu is after Thanksgiving when you have leftover turkey on hand and house guests to feed. However, Kentucky Hot Browns are so good you may want to roast a turkey breast just to make this recipe; I have included those instructions as well.

DOWN HOME COMFORT

Ruby Slipper Sippers

Mixed Greens with Vinaigrette, Bacon,
Sliced Eggs and Cranberries

Kentucky Hot Browns

Cinnamon and Pecan Roasted Apples

Cinnamon Rolls

RUBY SLIPPER SIPPERS

A refreshing drink with lots of color.

1 ½ cups fresh or frozen cranberries
1 cup cranberry juice cocktail
1 cup sugar
Juice and rind of 2 oranges
1 liter lemon-lime carbonated soda
Garnish: Whole cranberries

Pulse cranberries and cranberry juice in a food processor until berries are coarsely chopped. Place berries and remaining ingredients except lemon-lime soda in a saucepan over medium heat and cook 10 minutes. Strain. Cool cranberry syrup to room temperature. If desired, rub rims of glasses with lemon wedge and dip in sugar. Pour 1 to 2 tablespoons cranberry syrup into glasses and top with lemon-lime soda. Garnish with whole cranberries. Makes 8 servings

MIXED GREENS WITH VINAIGRETTE, BACON, SLICED EGGS AND DRIED CRANBERRIES

Vinaigrette
½ cup rice vinegar
¼ cup sugar
½ cup vegetable or canola oil
1 tablespoon chopped green onion
1 teaspoon Worcestershire sauce
1 teaspoon Dijon mustard
½ teaspoon salt
Fresh ground black pepper to taste

12 cups washed and broken into bite-size greens (romaine, spinach, baby greens)
1 cup sliced fresh mushrooms
4 eggs, hard-cooked, peeled and sliced
Garnish: Toasted sliced almonds and dried cranberries

1. **Combine** all vinaigrette ingredients in a plastic container and shake well. Place greens and mushrooms in a large bowl. Pour enough dressing over greens to lightly coat; toss to mix.

2. **Place** salad mixture on salad plates. Top each with egg slices, toasted almonds and a sprinkling of dried cranberries. Drizzle with additional dressing if desired. Makes 6 to 8 servings

Bonnie's Tip:
To toast almonds, place them in a single layer on a rimmed baking sheet. Toast in a preheated 350°F oven for 7 to 10 minutes or until golden.

CINNAMON AND PECAN ROASTED APPLES

The cinnamon candies give these apples a rosy glow and fabulous flavor.

6 large baking apples (Gala, Granny Smith, or Rome Beauty)
½ cup heavy cream
½ cup sugar

Filling
⅓ cup cinnamon candies (Red Hots™)
½ cup chopped pecans
¼ cup sugar
¼ cup butter

1. With a thin paring knife or apple corer, core the apples to within ¼ inch of the bottoms. Brush apples with heavy cream and roll in sugar. Place the apples in a baking dish, evenly spaced, not touching.

2. Loosely fill each apple center with a teaspoon or two of cinnamon candies. Then add a teaspoon of chopped pecans to each apple. Then fill each apple center with 2 teaspoons sugar, which will sift through the pecans. Top each apple with a pat of butter, pressing it slightly into the cavity. Fill the baking dish with ¼ inch of water.

3. Bake at 350°F for 30 to 40 minutes, or until apples are tender. Makes 6 servings

Red Hots were created in the early 1930s by the Ferrara Pan Candy Company. The name "cinnamon imperials" is a generic name used by the candy industry to indicate a piece of cinnamon hard candy such as Red Hots, which is a registered trademark of Ferrara Pan Candy.

CLASSIC KENTUCKY HOT BROWNS

An open-faced turkey sandwich that is heavenly. I first made this for a brunch after Thanksgiving just to use up the turkey breast, and my friends raved about it for weeks. The response was the same when I made it in a cooking class. It created such a buzz, I had to repeat the class for those who missed it!

I have been known to roast a turkey breast just for this recipe. The method I use is on the following page for roasting the breast.

Mushrooms
3 tablespoons butter
2 tablespoons minced onion
12 ounces mushrooms, cleaned and sliced
½ teaspoon salt
¼ teaspoon black pepper
1 tablespoon chopped fresh parsley

Sauce
¼ cup butter
¼ cup flour
2 cups whole milk
Pinch nutmeg
½ to ¾ teaspoon salt
⅛ teaspoon black pepper
⅛ teaspoon ground red pepper
2 cups grated sharp white Cheddar cheese,
    divided use
¼ cup grated Parmesan cheese

8 thick slices home-style white
    bread (like Pepperidge Farm),
    toasted
16 ounces thinly sliced turkey breast
8 slices bacon, cooked until crisp
Garnish: finely chopped scallions
    or chives, parsley or chopped
    tomato (optional)

1. For the Mushrooms: Heat butter in skillet and add onions, cook for 30 seconds. Add mushrooms, salt and pepper. Cook, stirring, until mushrooms begin to color and the liquid has evaporated. Stir in parsley, set aside.

2. For the Sauce: In a medium saucepan, melt butter over medium-high heat. Add the flour and cook, stirring until it bubbles. Add the milk, whisking constantly until it comes to a boil and is thick and smooth, about 3 to 4 minutes. Season with nutmeg, salt, black pepper and ground red pepper. Add 1 cup of the Cheddar cheese and the Parmesan cheese, stirring until melted. Remove from heat.

3. To assemble: Preheat boiler and place rack in top position. Place the toasted bread on a foil-lined baking sheet and run under broiler 20 seconds on both sides just to warm a bit. Divide the turkey among the toasted bread, top with mushrooms and ladle sauce over the top, spreading out to the edge. Sprinkle with remaining cheese.

4. Place under broiler until bubbly and the cheese starts to brown, 1 to 3 minutes -- watch carefully. Remove from oven. Transfer to plates. Cut each bacon slice in half and arrange over top of hot brown. Garnish as desired. Serve immediately. Makes 8 servings

Roasted Turkey Breast
Sometimes when I make Classic Kentucky Hot Browns for a large group, I will roast a turkey breast. If I have leftover turkey, I enjoy some turkey sandwiches a day or so later.

1 (4 to 5-pound) boneless turkey breast, thawed
¼ cup butter, room temperature
½ teaspoon rubbed sage or poultry seasoning
Salt and ground black pepper
¼ cup butter

Preheat oven to 425°F. Mix butter, sage, salt and pepper together and rub over breast. Place in a small roasting pan or skillet, and roast for 15 minutes. Reduce the heat to 350°F and continue roasting until an instant reading thermometer registers 165°F, about 1 ½ hours. Remove from oven, loosely tent with foil and let rest at least 15 minutes before carving.   (May be roasted ahead and refrigerated.)

WHY IS THIS CALLED A "HOT BROWN"?

THE STORY GOES *that in the 1920s, the Brown Hotel in Louisville, KY, would draw more than 1,200 guests to its evening dinner dance. In the wee hours of the morning, the hungry weary dancers would land in the restaurant. As a variation to the traditional ham and eggs, the Chef created a satisfying open-faced turkey sandwich with bacon and a delicate Mornay sauce, and the Hot Brown was born!*

THE HOT BROWN *is a distinctive Southern dish yet it can be found made many ways. The version here is my favorite and follows the traditional one made by Chef Fred Schmidt featuring turkey, bacon and mushrooms; however, I did garnish with tomatoes and fresh herbs. The Hot Brown now has many variations: It can be made with sliced or diced chicken, turkey, bacon or ham, and any combination of these ingredients. The bread may also be rye, pumpernickel or white. These open faced sandwiches are unquestionably a delicious regional dish that you should try.*

HOMEMADE CINNAMON ROLLS

Nothing makes the house smell better than freshly baked cinnamon rolls. You can bake these the day you mix the dough, or the shaped rolls may be covered and refrigerated, then baked the next day.

Dough
¼ cup water, warm (98 to 110°F)
1 package instant dry yeast (or 1 tablespoon if measuring from larger container)
¾ cup warm milk (98 to 110°F)
¼ cup sugar
1 large egg, room temperature
¼ cup butter, room temperature (or Crisco)
1 teaspoons salt
3 ½ to 3 ¾ cups all-purpose flour, plus additional for dusting
1 teaspoons salt
Vegetable oil or cooking spray

Filling
½ cup brown sugar
½ cup sugar
1 tablespoon ground cinnamon
3 tablespoons butter, room temperature

Icing
3 tablespoons cream or milk
1 ½ cups powdered sugar (a little more or less)
½ teaspoon vanilla or almond flavoring

Bonnie's Tip:
I admonish my students not to kill the yeast. Yeast is a tiny living plant that needs warm water for best results. Too hot and the yeast will die. Too cool and it will not rise sufficiently. It likes a warm, liquid environment between 98°F and 110°F.

Make sure, too, that the yeast is not outdated. If it does not become foamy, the dough will not rise.

1. For the Dough: Stir yeast into warm water between 98°F and 110°F. Add 2 teaspoons of the sugar. Stir and let set a few minutes until foamy. In the bowl of a stand mixer with the paddle attachment, whisk the warm milk, sugar, egg and butter. Add the yeast mixture.

2. Add approximately 2 cups of the flour and salt to the mixer bowl. Beat on low until moistened and combined, then increase speed to medium and beat for a couple of minutes to develop the gluten.

3. Remove the paddle attachment and replace with a dough hook. Add all but ¾ cup of the remaining flour and knead on medium-low speed for 4 to 5 minutes. Check the consistency of the dough and add more flour if necessary. The dough should feel soft and moist but not sticky. Knead on low speed until dough is very smooth and elastic and most of the dough forms a mass around the dough hook, cleaning the sides of the bowl.

4. Turn the dough out onto a lightly floured work surface; knead by hand about 30 seconds. Lightly oil a large bowl. Place dough in the bowl, lightly oil the top of the dough, cover and let double in volume, 2 to 2 ½ hours.

5. For the Filling: Combine the sugars and cinnamon in a medium bowl. Mix well; set aside.

6. Butter a 9 x 13-inch-pan. Turn the dough out onto a lightly floured work surface. Roll into an 18 x 12-inch-rectangle. Brush the top with melted butter, leaving ½ inch border along the long edge. Sprinkle the filling mixture over the dough, leaving a ¾ inch border along the top edge. Beginning with the long edge nearest you, roll the dough into a tight cylinder. Firmly pinch the seam to seal and roll the cylinder seam side down. Very gently squeeze the cylinder to create even thickness. Using a serrated knife or dental floss, slice the cylinder into 1 ½ inch slices; yielding 12 rolls.

Arrange rolls cut side down in the baking pan; cover with plastic wrap and store in the refrigerator overnight. (Or, you may choose to let rolls rise for an hour or so and bake right away. To bake the day you make the rolls, cover pan loosely with plastic wrap and allow rolls to rise for an hour or until they have doubled in size. Proceed with directions in step 8.)

7. If stored in the refrigerator, remove the rolls from the refrigerator and place in an oven that is turned off. Fill a shallow pan two-thirds full of boiling water and set on the rack below the rolls. Close the oven door and let the rolls rise until they look slightly puffy; approximately 30 to 45 minutes. Remove the rolls and the shallow pan of water from the oven.

8. Preheat the oven to 350°F. When the oven is ready, place the rolls on the middle rack and bake until golden brown, approximately 20 minutes.

9. For the Icing: While the rolls are cooling slightly, make the icing by whisking the cream, powdered sugar and vanilla or almond flavoring in a small, deep bowl. You may need to adjust consistency by adding additional powdered sugar or cream. Spread over the rolls. Serve warm or room temperature. Makes 12 rolls

COME *to* BRUNCH

A weekend brunch is a lovely way to entertain. It is early in the day; people tend to be more relaxed and will enjoy leisurely visiting over the meal. Your guests are bound to savor the Chicken Florentine Phyllo Pie, as it is not the usual brunch fare. It is delicious and looks gorgeous on a plate.

This is no doubt one of my favorite brunches. Each one of the parts is delicious on its own; but together, it makes one fantastic menu. The Chicken Florentine Phyllo Pie is made in a springform pan. When the sides are released, it can be transferred to a platter for a stunning entrée. The Blueberry Lemon Bundt Cake is moist and tangy with grated lemon zest and dotted with fresh, juicy blueberries.

COME TO BRUNCH

Festive Fresh Fruit Salad

Cranberry Streusel Muffins

Chicken Florentine Phyllo Pie

Deviled Eggs with Ham

Blueberry Lemon Bundt Cake

FESTIVE FRESH FRUIT SALAD

Orange Almond Sauce
1 ¼ cups sugar
3 tablespoons fresh lemon juice
¼ teaspoon salt
1 cup water
¼ cup amaretto (almond liqueur)
2 tablespoons orange-flavored liqueur (Grand Marnier or Triple Sec)

4 oranges
4 medium pears
2 cups seedless green grapes
2 cups seedless red grapes
4 kiwi fruit
1 cup strawberries
2 bananas

1. In a 2-quart saucepan over medium heat, combine sugar, lemon juice, salt and water and cook for 5 to 10 minutes, or until mixture becomes a light syrup. Stir in amaretto and orange-flavored liqueur. Refrigerate until syrup is cool.

2. When sauce is cool, peel and section oranges. Core and slice pears. In a large bowl, combine oranges, pears and grapes. Pour chilled sauce over fruit. Cover and refrigerate until well chilled, stirring occasionally.

3. To serve, peel and slice kiwi fruit. Stem strawberries, cut in half. Slice banana into thick slices. Gently stir into fruit mixture. Makes 10 to 12 servings

CRANBERRY STREUSEL MUFFINS

I really enjoy making and serving these when fresh cranberries are available, but dried ones will work, too.

Streusel Topping
⅓ cup brown sugar
½ teaspoon ground cinnamon
1 tablespoon unsalted butter
½ cup chopped walnuts

Muffins
2 ½ cups flour
1 teaspoon baking soda
2 teaspoons baking powder
½ teaspoon cinnamon
¼ teaspoon salt
1 ⅓ cups brown sugar, packed firm
⅔ cup vegetable oil
2 teaspoons grated orange rind
1 egg
1 cup buttermilk
2 teaspoons vanilla extract
1 ½ cups fresh cranberries, coarsely chopped (or 1 cup dried cranberries)

1. For the Topping: Mix sugar and cinnamon in a small bowl. Using a fork or pastry blender, blend butter into sugar. Stir in nuts; set aside.

2. For the Muffins: Adjust rack to middle position and preheat oven to 400°F. Lightly grease a 12-cup muffin pan or use paper liners. Whisk flour with baking soda, baking powder, cinnamon and salt. Set aside.

3. Stir together brown sugar, vegetable oil, orange rind and egg in a bowl. Whisk in buttermilk and vanilla. Gently stir dry ingredients into wet ingredients to blend. Fold in cranberries.

4. Fill muffin cups three-fourths full. Sprinkle streusel topping over batter in each muffin cup. Bake 15 minutes at 400°F; reduce heat to 350°F and bake until muffins are golden brown, 10 to 12 minutes. Let muffins cool in pan for 5 minutes; then transfer them to a wire rack to finish cooling. Makes 1 dozen large muffins

Bonnie's Tip:
If using dried cranberries, soften by soaking 5 to 10 minutes in hot water to plump them. If using fresh cranberries, you might want to freeze them partially so they do not discolor the batter.

To chop fresh cranberries, place in the food processor and pulse only a few times until coarsely chopped.

CHICKEN FLORENTINE PHYLLO PIE

Some have declared this is the best thing I have ever made. I'm not sure if that is true or not, but everyone does enjoy it. It is a beautiful thing when done, and makes an astonishing entrée for lunch or brunch. This can be made a day in advance and baked shortly before serving.

1 tablespoon olive oil
1 small onion, chopped
2 cloves garlic, minced
2 cups cooked, fresh spinach, coarsely chopped, drained and squeezed dry (or 1 [10-ounce] package Birdseye frozen chopped spinach, thawed, drained and squeezed dry)
1 (8-ounce) carton ricotta cheese
4 ounces feta cheese
¼ cup freshly grated Parmesan cheese
3 eggs, lightly beaten

1 teaspoon dried thyme
⅛ teaspoon ground red pepper
20 sheets (about ½ pound) frozen phyllo pastry, thawed, two sheets reserved for top
1 cup butter, melted (or butter-flavored cooking spray)
2 tablespoons dry bread crumbs
3 cups cooked, chopped chicken
1 ½ cup mayonnaise (prefer Hellmann's)
½ teaspoon curry powder

1. Heat olive oil in skillet over medium heat; sauté onion and garlic until transclucent. Stir spinach, ricotta cheese, feta cheese, Parmesan cheese, eggs and seasonings into skillet, mixing well. Set aside.

2. Coat a 9-inch-springform pan with cooking spray. Place 2 sheets of phyllo on counter top, keeping remaining sheets covered. Lightly brush butter or spray with cooking spray one sheet of phyllo; overlap the second sheet by 3 inches on short edge to form a large square; brush butter or spray surface with the spray. This large square is the shape you want to make a pastry layer that will fit the pan. Repeat layering and buttering (or spraying with butter flavored spray) two sheets at a time, adding layers to the square. Continue until only two sheets remain; keep them covered for now. Gently press the large square of pastry layers just created into the pan, forming a shell with the edges hanging over the pan. Sprinkle bread crumbs on bottom of shell. Fill phyllo shell with the spinach-cheese mixture, spreading all the way to the pan edges. Place chicken in an even layer over spinach-cheese layer.

3. Combine mayonnaise and curry powder; spread mayonnaise over chicken. To make the top lid on the phyllo pie, butter or spray the remaining two phyllo sheets, stacking them on top of each other; then fold in half, making four layers. Place it on top of the filling, tucking top sheets down around filling. Fold over-hanging edges over top. Brush butter or spray top with cooking spray, coating the entire surface. Don't be alarmed if it doesn't look "tidy", as it will be lovely after it bakes.

4. Bake uncovered at 400°F for 25 minutes. Cover loosely with foil so the top will not over-brown. Continue to bake an additional 30 minutes. Remove foil. Let stand 10 minutes. Remove rim from pan carefully and transfer to serving platter. Serve warm; cut into 8 wedges. Makes 8 servings

Bonnie's Tip:
I often use a butter-flavored spray as it is quicker and makes a lighter product. Most people cannot tell the difference! But if you are a purist, by all means melt the butter and spread it on each layer. Either way is lovely.

Working with phyllo can be a challenge. Remove all the sheets you need, cover them with a layer of plastic wrap and then a towel to prevent drying out.

To thaw frozen phyllo dough, remove from freezer and place in refrigerator overnight or place on the counter for 3 or 4 hours. Do not open until you are ready to use it so it will not dry out.

Chicken Florentine Phyllo Pie, p. 194

DEVILED EGGS WITH HAM

Everyone loves deviled eggs. This version is stuffed with ham, which makes an interesting variation. These are also good served at parties.

Ham Filling
2 ½ cups cubed lean cooked ham
6 ounces cream cheese
3 green onions, sliced
1 teaspoon Dijon mustard
Tabasco sauce to taste
¼ to ⅓ cup mayonnaise (prefer Hellmann's)
¼ cup butter

8 hard boiled eggs
Garnish: Parsley or alfalfa sprouts

1. For the Filling: Place ham in food processor with metal blade. Process with on and off motions until chopped. Transfer ham to a bowl. Place cream cheese, onions, mustard and Tabasco in food processor bowl. Process until cream cheese is soft and smooth. Return ham to processor bowl. Add ¼ cup mayonnaise. Process until blended and smooth. If desired, thin mixture with additional mayonnaise.

2. To assemble eggs: Cut eggs in half lengthwise. Discard yolks (or give to the cat). Pipe ham mixture into eggs. Cover and chill until serving time. Arrange on bed of alfalfa sprouts. Makes 16

Bonnie's Tip:
To properly boil eggs, place room-temperature eggs in a heavy saucepan. Add cold water until there is one inch of water above eggs.

Place over medium heat; bring to a rolling boil. Remove eggs from heat. Cover and let stand 20 minutes in hot water. Drain.

Chill immediately by immersing eggs in ice water. Peel eggs; place in a container. Cover with ice and water; cover container and refrigerate until ready to use. Eggs will keep 3 to 4 days this way; change the water daily.

BLUEBERRY LEMON BUNDT CAKE

This is a beautiful blueberry-lemon cake that has a moist texture and very tender crumb. Dust it with powdered sugar, glaze it or just enjoy it plain with a cup of coffee or tea.

2 ¾ cups flour
1 ½ teaspoons baking powder
¼ teaspoon baking soda
½ teaspoon salt
1 cup butter, room temperature
1 ¾ cups sugar
4 eggs
2 tablespoons fresh lemon juice
1 tablespoon lemon zest
1 teaspoon vanilla extract
1 cup buttermilk
1 ¼ cups fresh blueberries, rinsed, tossed
    with 1 tablespoon flour
Lemon Glaze (optional)

1. Heat oven to 350°F. Butter and flour a 12-cup bundt pan.

2. Combine flour, baking powder, baking soda and salt in a large bowl. Set aside.

3. In mixer bowl, cream butter until smooth with electric mixer. Add sugar and beat for 2 to 3 minutes until fluffy. Beat in eggs, one at a time, beating well after each addition. Add lemon juice, lemon zest and vanilla and beat until combined.

4. Add flour in three additions, alternating with buttermilk. Beat for 2 minutes. Gently fold in blueberries. Spoon into prepared pan, smoothing batter evenly in pan.

5. Bake at 350°F for 50 to 60 minutes or until a toothpick inserted in center of cake comes out clean. Cool 15 minutes on a wire rack. Carefully loosen the edges of the cake with a small thin knife, invert on cake plate and remove pan. Serve plain, or dust with powdered sugar or drizzle with lemon glaze if desired.

Lemon Glaze
1 ½ cups powdered sugar
3 to 4 tablespoons fresh lemon juice
Garnish: Lemon zest

Combine powdered sugar and 3 tablespoons fresh lemon juice in a small bowl. Add more juice if needed. Drizzle over cake. Garnish with lemon zest. Makes 12 to 16 servings

The APPETIZER PARTY

Party appetizers, hors d'oeuvres, finger foods--whatever you want to call them, they are not just little, before-dinner treats any more. These appetizers can carry the party all by themselves and look good doing it.

Whether you are hosting a party or contributing to one, you will want to check out these recipes. It is an outstanding selection and you can issue those invitations with confidence!

THE APPETIZER PARTY

Mediterranean Layered Dip
Legendary Crab Rounds

Shrimp Shooters with
Spicy Dipping Sauce

Thai-Style Chicken Salad
in Wonton Cups

Rosemary Spiced Nuts

Warm Spinach Dip with Toasted
Baguette Slices

Hot Ham Canapés with Raspberry
Chipotle Sauce

New Potatoes Stuffed with Bacon,
Cheese and Chives

Goat Cheese with Sun-Dried
Tomatoes and Rosemary

Savory Smoked Salmon Torte

Ultimate Cranberry Bars

Chocolate Babycakes

MEDITERRANEAN LAYERED DIP

Make this showy dip and then watch it disappear! A party favorite every time I serve it.

Vegetable Mixture
2 medium tomatoes, seeded and chopped
1 small English cucumber, peeled and chopped
1 small red or yellow bell pepper, seeded and chopped
1 tablespoon chopped fresh parsley
2 tablespoons extra virgin olive oil
1 tablespoon red wine vinegar
½ teaspoon salt
¼ teaspoon crushed red pepper flakes

3 cups hummus (commercially prepared or home-made)
2 cups shredded fresh spinach
4 ounces feta cheese, crumbled
½ cup sliced green onions
¼ cup chopped, pitted Kalamata olives
Optional: 2 tablespoons pistachio nuts
Pita chips

1. **Combine** vegetable mixture in a bowl; stir to mix. Cover and set aside for 30 minutes for flavors to marry.

2. **Spread** hummus on a large serving platter. Arrange spinach on top, leaving a 1-inch-border of hummus.

3. **Drain** excess liquid from vegetable mixture; discard liquid. Spoon vegetable mixture over spinach, leaving a ½ inch border of spinach. Sprinkle feta cheese over vegetable layer.

4. **Top** with green onions, Kalamata olives and pistachio nuts. Serve with pita chips.
Makes 12 to 14 servings

Shrimp Shooters with Spicy Dipping Sauce, p. 201

SHRIMP SHOOTERS WITH SPICY DIPPING SAUCE

If you don't like too much "heat" in your food, start with the lesser amount of the chipotle. It carries a powerful punch!

1 pound jumbo cooked, shrimp, peeled but tails left intact

Spicy Dipping Sauce
1 tablespoon Hoisin sauce
1 tablespoon honey
½ to 1 chipotle pepper in adobo sauce, minced
2 teaspoons lime juice
⅓ cup finely chopped cilantro
1 cup regular or light mayonnaise
Garnish: Fresh cilantro

1. **Rinse** the shrimp well; drain. Chill until serving time.

2. **For the Sauce:** Combine Hoisin sauce, honey, chipotle pepper, and lime juice in a small bowl. Stir to combine. Add cilantro and mayonnaise. Stir until well mixed. Cover and chill.

3. **To serve:** Place a couple teaspoons of sauce in shot glasses and hang shrimp by tail on rim of glass. Garnish with cilantro if desired. Makes approximately 30 pieces

Bonnie's Tip:
You will find canned chipotle chiles in adobo sauce in the Hispanic area of most large supermarkets.

You will probably only use one or two out of the can. To freeze them for later use, spread them on a parchment- or plastic-lined baking sheet in a single layer. Freeze until firm. When frozen, store in a zipper-type storage bag or freezer container and you will be able to pull out one or two as needed.

LEGENDARY CRAB ROUNDS

This recipe has been a favorite of mine for many years; and I even included it in my earlier cookbook, Cooking from the Heartland. It is quick to assemble with few ingredients and everyone loves it.

½ cup mayonnaise (prefer Hellmann's)
2 tablespoons finely chopped onion
½ cup shredded Cheddar cheese
¼ teaspoon Tabasco
⅛ teaspoon curry powder
¼ pound crab meat, chopped and thoroughly drained
French baguette, sliced into ½-inch-thick-slices

1. **Combine** mayonnaise, onion, cheese, Tabasco, and curry powder in a mixing bowl. Stir until well mixed. Fold in crab meat.

2. **Shortly** before serving, place bread rounds on baking sheets. Spoon crab mixture on bread rounds, spreading a thin layer to the edges.

3. **Place** oven rack in the top position close to the broiler unit. Preheat broiler. Broil crab rounds until golden brown. Watch carefully—it only takes a couple of minutes. Serve hot. Makes about 25 pieces

ROSEMARY SPICED NUTS

There are several variations of this recipe; some also include brown sugar for a sweet-hot taste. I prefer this one and really like the flavor when made with fresh rosemary.

3 cups nuts (mixed nuts or your favorite kind)
3 tablespoons melted butter
2 teaspoons dried rosemary or 2 tablespoons fresh, minced rosemary
¾ teaspoon ground red pepper
½ teaspoon kosher salt

Preheat oven to 350°F. Melt butter in a glass measure on High for 15 seconds in the microwave or until melted. Stir in rosemary, ground red pepper and salt. Pour over nuts, tossing until well coated. Place nuts on parchment lined baking sheet. Roast in preheated oven for 10 to 12 minutes. Cool and enjoy.

THAI-STYLE CHICKEN SALAD IN WONTON CUPS

These are beautiful and delicious and a nice addition to any festive occasion.

Wonton Cups
24 wonton wrappers
Melted butter

Chicken Salad
¼ cup fresh lime juice
1 teaspoon salt
1 teaspoon Thai fish sauce
½ teaspoon chili powder
¼ cup finely chopped fresh cilantro
½ teaspoon sugar
3 cups cooked, finely chopped, chicken breast
⅓ cup minced green onions
¼ cup chopped roasted peanuts
¼ cup mayonnaise, or to taste
Optional garnish: Chopped red bell pepper

Bonnie's Tip:
I usually make a lot of the wonton cups in advance when I am going to be serving this. The prepared cups keep well in a dry, air-tight container.

1. For the Wonton Cups: Preheat oven to 375°F. Brush wonton wrappers with butter. Press into mini-muffin tins. Bake for 5 to 8 minutes or until crispy and golden. Cool. Store in airtight container until ready to use.

2. For the Thai-Style Chicken Salad: Combine lime juice, salt, fish sauce, chili powder, cilantro and sugar. Stir into chicken. Add green onions and peanuts. Add enough mayonnaise to moisten. (May be made a day in advance, covered and refrigerated). Fill wonton cups shortly before serving. Makes 24 pieces

WARM SPINACH DIP WITH TOASTED BAGUETTE SLICES

Spinach dip is always popular—it's warm, oozing with cheese and invites camaraderie and sharing. My version is flavored with sherry and uses Monterrey Jack cheese for its smooth flavor and texture.

4 tablespoons vegetable oil
½ small onion, chopped
2 garlic cloves, minced
3 tablespoons flour
½ cup chicken broth
½ cup heavy cream or half-and-half
2 tablespoons dry sherry, optional
4 cups (6 ounces) fresh spinach leaves, washed
1 ¼ cups Parmesan cheese
2 cups shredded Monterey Jack cheese
¼ cup sour cream
¼ to ½ teaspoon ground red pepper

Baguette slices, toasted

1. Heat oil in heavy large pot over medium heat. Add onion and garlic; sauté until onion is tender, about 6 minutes. Add flour, cook for a minute or two. Add broth, cream and sherry. Bring to a boil, stirring constantly. Cook until mixture thickens, stirring frequently. Stir in spinach; cook until spinach is wilted. Stir in Parmesan cheese.

2. Transfer to food processor or blender. (If using a blender, cover but leave center cap off and place a clean dish towel over the opening as you want to allow the steam to escape. If you are using a food processor, this will already be accomplished with the feed tube.) Process until spinach is finely chopped. Add Monterey Jack cheese. Pulse until blended and melted. Add sour cream and ground red pepper. Taste and adjust seasonings if needed. Transfer dip to bowl. Serve warm with toasted baguette slices.   Makes 3 cups

HOT HAM CANAPÉS WITH RASPBERRY CHIPOTLE SAUCE

The contrasting flavors of the salty ham with the sweet, spicy Raspberry Chipotle Sauce makes this canapé irresistible.

Bonnie's Tip:
This is a warm canapé that is easy to prepare and serve, as both the ham mixture and the sauce may be prepared 2 days in advance.

8 ounces good-quality ham (such as Hillshire Farms or Hormel 81)
1 cup mayonnaise (prefer Hellmann's)
½ cup thinly sliced green onions
½ teaspoon dry mustard
¼ teaspoon Tabasco Sauce

½ cup shredded sharp Cheddar cheese
½ cup shredded Monterey Jack cheese
Garnish: Raspberry Chipotle sauce, minced fresh parsley or cilantro
1 French baguette, sliced ½ inch thick

1. Place ham in food processor. Pulse off and on until ham is coarsely chopped. Add remaining ingredients, and pulse a few times just until mixed. Don't over do this—we need a little texture. (This may be made in advance. Place in covered container and refrigerate for a day or so.)

2. Shortly before serving, place bread rounds on cookie sheets. Spoon mixture on bread rounds. Place oven rack in the top position close to the broiler. Broil until golden. Watch carefully, it only takes a couple of minutes.

3. Before serving drizzle with Raspberry Chipotle Sauce. Add a bit of minced parsley if desired. Makes about 30 pieces

Raspberry Chipotle Sauce
1 cup frozen raspberries, thawed
2 tablespoons sugar
1 tablespoon Hoisin sauce
1 tablespoon chopped chipotle

In a microwave-safe container, heat raspberries, sugar, Hoisin and chipotle until it simmers and sugar is dissolved. Puree in food processor or blender; strain into a small bowl. (May be made 2 or 3 days in advance) Cool before using.

NEW POTATOES STUFFED WITH BACON, CHEESE AND CHIVES

These are always popular—my version is loaded!

Bonnie's Tip:
Fill a disposable pastry bag with the potato mixture and pipe it into the hollowed out potatoes. This makes a decorative top that looks very pretty on a tray, and is also much quicker than spooning it into the shells.

15 small, new potatoes
2 tablespoons sour cream
4 bacon slices, cooked until crisp, then crumbled
2 tablespoons minced chives or green onions

Salt and pepper
Shredded Cheddar cheese
Garnish: Minced parsley, chopped pimiento, red or black caviar

1. Boil potatoes until just tender. Cool. Cut in half. Scoop out centers. Combine centers from potatoes, sour cream, bacon and chives in mixing bowl. Season to taste with salt and pepper. Beat until blended. Spoon or pipe mixture into center of potatoes. Sprinkle top with shredded cheese.

2. Arrange on baking sheet. Place under preheated broiler and broil until heated through and cheese on top has melted. If desired, decorate tops with fresh parsley, chopped pimiento or caviar. Makes 30 pieces

GOAT CHEESE WITH SUN-DRIED TOMATOES AND ROSEMARY

The color combination of this is amazing. The white cheese topped with the colorful red tomatoes and fresh green rosemary—it looks much more impressive than the sum of its parts.

½ cup dried tomato halves (packed in oil), drained
1 garlic clove
2 tablespoons olive oil

1 tablespoon chopped fresh rosemary
1 (11-ounce) package goat cheese
Garnish: Fresh rosemary
Assorted crackers

1. Chop dried tomatoes. Combine with garlic, oil and rosemary. Cover and chill for 1 to 8 hours.

2. Place goat cheese on serving tray. Spoon tomato mixture over top. Garnish with fresh rosemary sprigs. Serve with assorted crackers. Makes 8 servings

SAVORY SMOKED SALMON TORTE

This makes a large torte (9-inch) but can be made into two smaller ones (6-inch) as well. It must be made a day or two in advance, which is a great benefit when entertaining.

½ cup dried bread crumbs
2 pounds (32 ounces) cream cheese, room temperature
4 eggs
1 ½ cups shredded sharp Cheddar cheese
¾ cup thinly sliced green onions
½ teaspoon grated lemon zest (rind)

½ teaspoon salt
⅛ teaspoon ground red pepper
1 cup sour cream
6 ounces smoked salmon, chopped
Garnish: Sour cream, black olives, chopped red bell pepper, fresh parsley
Accompaniment: Assorted crackers

1. Preheat oven to 350°F. Butter bottom and sides of a 9-inch-springform pan. Dust with dry bread crumbs; shake out excess. Wrap in a double thickness of foil to make it waterproof. Set aside.

2. Beat cream cheese until smooth. Beat in eggs, one at a time. Add cheese, green onions, lemon zest, salt and pepper. Mix well. Fold in sour cream and smoked salmon.

3. Pour batter into prepared pan. Set springform pan in a baking pan and place in oven. Pour hot water in baking pan until it comes about half way up the sides of the spring form pan. Bake 45 minutes. Turn oven off; do not open the door and leave torte in oven for 60 minutes. Remove torte from pan of water; remove foil and cool on a rack. Cover top and chill for 8 hours.

4. Unmold and garnish as desired. Serve at room temperature with assorted crackers. Makes 15 to 20 servings

Bonnie's Tip:
Use hot smoked salmon in this for best flavor. This is nice to serve a large group. Elevate the torte by placing on a stemmed cake plate, garnishing lavishly and serving with assorted crackers. It is both beautiful and delicious.

ULTIMATE CRANBERRY BARS

*A beautiful bar cookie with the cranberry layer peeking through a generous drizzle of white chocolate. Decadent and delicious! I first made these for an Open House when I opened **Cooking at Bonnie's Place**. They quickly gained lots of attention so I taught a class on how to make them. The recipe makes a very large batch—but that is good as you will have some to share and perhaps some to freeze for later.*

Base
2 cups all-purpose flour
½ cup packed light brown sugar
½ teaspoon salt
¾ cup cold butter, cut into ½ inch cubes

Topping
1 cup butter
1 ⅔ cups granulated sugar
¼ cup light corn syrup
½ teaspoon salt
2 ½ cups fresh or frozen cranberries, coarsely chopped
1 teaspoon vanilla
1 ½ cups pecans (12 ounces), toasted and cooled, then coarsely chopped
Garnish: 2 ounces white chocolate, finely chopped
Special equipment: candy thermometer

Bonnie's Tip:
To toast pecans, place on a shallow baking sheet and place in a preheated 350°F oven for 6 to 8 minutes or until golden and fragrant.

1. For the Base: Preheat oven to 350°F. Line a 10 x 15-inch-shallow baking pan with foil, leaving a 2 inch overhang on the two short sides. Butter foil sides, but not the bottom.

2. Blend flour, brown sugar, and salt in a food processor, then add butter and pulse until mixture begins to form small (roughly pea-size) lumps. Sprinkle into baking pan, then press down firmly all over to form an even layer. Bake in middle of oven until golden and firm to the touch, 15 to 17 minutes, then cool in pan on a rack.

3. For the Topping: Melt butter in a 3-quart heavy saucepan over moderate heat and stir in sugar, corn syrup, and salt. Boil over moderately-high heat, stirring occasionally, until caramel registers 245°F on candy thermometer, about 8 minutes. Carefully stir in cranberries, then boil until caramel returns to 245°F. Remove from heat and stir in vanilla, then stir in pecans until well coated. Working quickly, spread caramel topping over base using a fork to distribute nuts and berries evenly. Cool completely.

4. Lift bars in foil from pan and transfer to a cutting board.

5. Place white chocolate in microwave-safe container and microwave on Medium-High for 30 seconds, stirring every 10 seconds until melted. Transfer chocolate to a small, disposable pastry bag. Snip off a small opening at the end. Pipe chocolate decoratively over top. Let stand at room temperature until chocolate sets, about 1 hour. Cut into small squares or bars. Makes 10 x 15-inch pan

CHOCOLATE BABYCAKES

These mini cakes are addictive. They are easy to make but watch carefully and do not overbake them so they will remain moist.

4 ounces unsweetened chocolate, broken into bits
½ cup (1 stick) butter, room temperature
2 cups sugar
4 eggs
2 teaspoons vanilla
¼ teaspoon salt
1 cup all purpose flour
1 cup walnuts or pecans, coarsely chopped

1. Preheat oven to 325°F. Line mini muffin pans with paper liners or spray bottoms with vegetable oil spray.

2. Heat chocolate and butter in microwave just until melted. Stir and set aside to cool.

3. In a large bowl, combine sugar, eggs, vanilla and salt; beat until light and smooth. Stir the chocolate mixture into the egg mixture. Add flour, stirring just enough to make the mixture smooth again. Fold in nuts.

4. Fill mini muffin pans three-quarters full; bake for 15 to 20 minutes until done. Remove from pan. Cool completely and remove paper liners when cooled. If desired, decorate tops with melted white or semisweet chocolate. (See step #5 in recipe on opposite page for technique.) Makes about 4 ½ dozen

Ultimate Cranberry Bars, p. 206

Elegant HOLIDAY DINNER

Set the table, light the candles and uncork the wine when you serve this beautiful menu. Your guests will savor every morsel. Much of it is made in advance so you will have time to enjoy your own dinner party.

Plan ahead and get organized and you can make this menu appear effortless. The Individual Beef Wellington recipe is not difficult but it is time consuming. Assemble it a few hours ahead of serving time and refrigerate it. Puff pastry must be chilled when it goes in the hot oven so you get the most rise from the dough. Plan to make the cheesecake a few days ahead; cover and refrigerate it.

ELEGANT HOLIDAY DINNER

Crab Cakes with Baby Greens and
Lemon Dill Vinaigrette

Individual Beef Wellingtons

Golden Potato Gratin
with Goat Cheese and Herbs

Sautéed Green Beans with Bacon,
Shallots and Mushrooms

Chocolate Glazed Irish Cream
Cheesecake

CRAB CAKES WITH BABY GREENS AND LEMON DILL VINAIGRETTE

Crab cakes benefit from being prepared a few hours ahead since the bread crumbs absorb the moisture and the flavors blend.

Bonnie's Tip:
For uniform crab cakes, use an ice cream scoop to place equal portions on a baking sheet. Then form into crab cakes. For beautiful crab cakes, mold each scoop of the mixture into a round cutter with an open top and you will have uniform, beautifully shaped cakes.

Crab Cakes
¼ cup mayonnaise (prefer Hellmann's)
¼ cup minced green onions
1 large egg
2 tablespoons fresh lemon juice
1 teaspoon dried dill weed
1 tablespoon Dijon mustard
1 teaspoon Old Bay Seasoning
¼ teaspoon ground black pepper
1 pound lump crabmeat
2 cups panko (Japanese breadcrumbs), divided use
2 to 3 tablespoons butter
2 to 3 tablespoons canola oil

12 cups mixed baby greens, washed and dried
1 cucumber, peeled and thinly sliced
¼ small red onion, cut into thin wedges
Lemon Dill Vinaigrette (recipe follows)
Garnish: Parmesan cheese (optional)

1. Line a baking sheet with parchment or waxed paper. In a large bowl, combine mayonnaise, green onions, egg, lemon juice, dill weed, mustard, Old Bay seasoning and black pepper and whisk together. Mix in crabmeat and 1 cup panko, breaking up crabmeat slightly. Let stand 10 minutes.

2. Place remaining panko on rimmed baking sheet, spreading slightly. Form crab mixture into sixteen 2-inch-diameter-patties, using about scant ¼ cup for each. Press both sides of patties into panko. Transfer patties to waxed-paper-lined baking sheet. Cover and chill at least 1 hour and up to 1 day.

3. Melt 1 tablespoon butter with 1 tablespoon oil in each of two heavy large skillets over medium-high heat. Add crab cakes to skillets and cook until golden on both sides, adding more butter and oil as needed, about 5 minutes total. Transfer to paper towel lined plate.

4. Place mixed greens, cucumber and red onion in large bowl. Toss with enough Lemon Dill Vinaigrette to coat. Divide greens among 10 plates. Place 2 crab cakes alongside greens on each plate. Drizzle each crab cake with 1 teaspoon vinaigrette before serving. Garnish with shaved or shredded Parmesan cheese if desired. Makes 10 servings

Lemon Dill Vinaigrette
½ cup vegetable oil
3 tablespoons fresh lemon juice
1 garlic clove, minced
1 tablespoon minced green onion
1 ½ teaspoons Dijon mustard
2 teaspoons sugar
½ teaspoon salt
½ teaspoon grated lemon peel
½ teaspoon dried dill weed
¼ teaspoon freshly ground black pepper

Whisk all ingredients in a bowl to blend. Taste and adjust seasonings if desired. May be made 2 days in advance. Cover and chill. Makes ¾ cup

Bonnie's Tip:
Frozen puff pastry is found in the frozen foods section of most large supermarkets. Working with frozen puff pastry is an easy way to make beautiful food. The pastry must not become warm while you are working with it. If it becomes warm and sticky, transfer it to the refrigerator until it is chilled and firm again. You will get the highest rise out of the pastry if it is cold when it goes into a hot oven.

INDIVIDUAL BEEF WELLINGTONS

A beautiful entrée that may be prepared in advance. Nice to serve with Horseradish Chive Sauce. This recipe may easily be doubled or tripled for a larger group.

4 beef tenderloin steaks, cut 1 ¼ inches thick (5 to 6 ounces)
1 tablespoon butter
½ onion, minced
8 ounces fresh mushrooms, finely chopped
1 clove garlic, minced
Salt and freshly ground black pepper to taste
¼ cup fresh parsley, finely chopped
½ (17-ounce) package frozen puff pastry sheets (prefer Pepperidge Farm)
About 1 tablespoon flour
¼ cup dry bread crumbs
1 egg beaten with 1 tablespoon water

1. Lightly brown steaks in a non-stick skillet over medium-high heat. Remove from skillet. Chill.

2. Heat butter in skillet over medium heat. Add onion, mushrooms and garlic. Cook until softened and wilted. Continue to cook until all the moisture has evaporated and mixture appears dry. Remove from heat. Season with salt and pepper. Stir in chopped parsley. Set aside. Cool completely.

3. Thaw frozen pastry by placing on countertop for 20 to 25 minutes or thaw overnight in refrigerator. Pastry should be thawed but still cold.

4. On a lightly floured surface, roll pastry sheet into a 14-inch square, then cut into four 7 inch squares. Remove one square inch from each corner. Sprinkle pastry center lightly with 1 tablespoon dry bread crumbs. Spread a layer of mushroom mixture over pastry squares to within ½ inch of edges. Place steak on top. Brush pastry edges with egg wash and wrap pastry around steak, pinching to seal edges.

5. Place on ungreased baking sheet, seam side down. Decorate tops with pastry trimmings if desired. Cover and chill. Pastry must be very cold when it goes into the oven. (May be covered and chilled up to 4 hours at this point.)

6. Place in preheated 400°F oven and bake for 20 to 25 minutes or until pastry is golden.

Horseradish Chive Sauce
½ cup mayonnaise (prefer Hellmann's)
½ cup sour cream
¼ cup chopped fresh chives or green onions
2 tablespoons prepared horseradish
2 tablespoons drained capers
Freshly ground black pepper

Combine all ingredients in a medium bowl. Season generously with freshly ground black pepper. Cover and refrigerate until ready to use. Makes about 2 cups sauce.

GOLDEN POTATO GRATIN WITH GOAT CHEESE AND HERBS

The creamy goat cheese and generous lacing of herbs creates a very flavorful gratin.

2 ¾ cups heavy cream
¾ cup chicken broth (homemade or canned)
½ small onion, finely chopped
1 clove garlic, minced
1 teaspoon dried basil
¼ teaspoon dried leaf thyme

¼ teaspoon dried oregano
¾ teaspoon salt
6 ounces fresh goat cheese
6 ounces cream cheese
4 pounds russet potatoes, peeled and thinly sliced
1 ½ cups shredded Gruyere cheese

1. Preheat oven to 400°F. Butter 13 x 9-inch-glass baking dish. Place cream, chicken broth, onion, garlic, basil, thyme, oregano and salt in a large pot. Bring to a simmer over medium-high heat. Add cheeses; whisk until smooth. Add potatoes to pot; return to simmer, then remove from heat.

2. Transfer potato mixture to prepared dish, spreading evenly. Sprinkle with Gruyere cheese. Cover with foil and bake 15 minutes. Uncover and bake until potatoes are very tender and liquid thickens, about 50 minutes. Cool 10 minutes before serving.
Makes 8 to 10 servings

Bonnie's Tip:
Russet potatoes are starchy and work well in this recipe. Do not rinse potato slices, as the water would remove the outer layer of starch that helps to thicken this dish.

SAUTÉED GREEN BEANS WITH BACON, SHALLOTS AND MUSHROOMS

Green beans and bacon are wonderful together, but the shallots and mushrooms put this one over the top!

3 pounds fresh green beans, ends trimmed
6 tablespoons butter
4 shallots, peeled and thinly sliced
1 pound mushrooms, sliced

2 tablespoons honey
1 tablespoon soy sauce
8 slices bacon, cooked crisp and set aside
Salt and pepper

1. Bring a large pot of water to a boil; add salt and fresh green beans. Cook until beans are just tender, about 6 to 10 minutes, depending upon the maturity of the green beans. Drain beans and rinse under cold water. Drain again.

2. Melt butter in a large, heavy skillet over medium high heat. Add shallots; cook 1 minute. Add mushrooms; cook until tender and moisture has evaporated. Stir in honey, soy sauce, green beans, and bacon. Cook, tossing constantly, until beans are heated through. Season with salt and pepper. Makes 8 to 12 servings

Bonnie's Tip:
Shallots are related to the onion family and tastes a bit like an onion. However, they are smaller, sweeter and milder in flavor and are used extensively in French cuisine.

CHOCOLATE GLAZED IRISH CREAM CHEESECAKE

I remember vividly the first time I demonstrated this cheesecake on television; it was during the 6 o'clock news on the local ABC-affiliated station. My segment went without a hitch, and the minute the program went to commercial, the anchor called over and asked me to save him a piece. The station was inundated with requests for this recipe.

1 ⅓ cups graham cracker crumbs
2 tablespoons sugar
⅓ cup butter, melted

4 (8-ounce) packages cream cheese,
　room temperature
1 ¼ cups sugar
4 large eggs
⅓ cup sour cream
⅓ cup Irish Cream liqueur (such as
　Bailey's)
1 teaspoon vanilla extract

Glaze
1 cup heavy whipping cream
2 tablespoons butter
2 tablespoons light corn syrup
9 ounces (1 ½ cups) semisweet or
　bittersweet chocolate chips
½ teaspoon vanilla extract

Bonnie's Tip:
When mixing the batter, do not beat the eggs too much or it may cause the cheesecake top to crack. Eggs are a leavening agent, causing the batter to rise. Then when the cake cools down, it deflates and is likely to crack.

1. For the Crust: Preheat oven to 350°F. Combine crust ingredients in a bowl, mixing well. Press onto bottom of 9 or 9 ½-inch-springform pan. Bake 10 minutes to set the crust. Cool. Wrap outside of pan in double layer of heavy-duty aluminum wrap to prevent leaking while cheesecake bakes in a hot water bath.

2. Beat cream cheese and sugar in large bowl until smooth and light. Add eggs, one at a time, beating just until combined. Mix in remaining ingredients.

3. Pour filling into crust. Set the cheesecake in a larger pan (i.e. roasting pan); place in preheated 350°F oven. Carefully pour hot water into larger pan until water comes half-way up the side of the cheesecake. Bake for 1 hour. Turn off oven without opening door; leave cheesecake in oven for 1 hour. Transfer cake to rack; cool to room temperature. Cover with plastic wrap and chill overnight.

4. For the Glaze: In a medium saucepan, heat the cream and butter cream, butter and syrup over low heat until the cream is very hot but not boiling. Remove the pan from the heat. Stir in the chocolate chips. Let stand for a minute to soften; then whisk the mixture until all of chocolate has melted. Stir in vanilla. Let cool slightly until warm but still will flow.

5. Release pan sides from cheesecake by running a sharp knife around pan to loosen cake. Place cheesecake on rack set over a baking sheet. Pour glaze over cheesecake, spreading with spatula to cover top and sides and allows excess to drip onto sheet. Refrigerate until glaze sets, about 30 minutes. (May be prepared 1 day ahead.) Transfer to platter.
Makes 12 servings

Bonnie's Tip:
Pressing the crumbs firmly on the bottom of the pan makes a firm crust that cuts nicely without crumbling. Place crumbs in the pan and cover with a piece of plastic wrap. If you have a flat tart pan bottom, use that to press the crumbs firmly in place. If that is not available, use your hands to press the crumbs firmly in the bottom. Then use a flat bottomed glass to go around the edges to pack the crumbs firmly. Remove the plastic wrap and continue with the recipe.

Acknowledgements

As I contemplate the many family members and friends who have actually helped me compile this book, I am overwhelmed with gratitude. Your generosity of time and talent are amazing; your encouragement, friendship and inspiration are actually components of this book.

The seeds of this book were planted by the hundreds of students who attended cooking classes in my home kitchen and then later at my cooking school. Because of their contagious enthusiasm, I continued to develop cooking classes with seasonal menus—and this cookbook is the result of those classes. My heartfelt thanks and gratitude for my culinary students who attended classes, contributed recipes or recipe concepts, cooked with me, laughed with me, and added much joy and purpose to my life.

Special Thanks

To Managing Editor, RoxAnn Banks Dicker, PhD, who encouraged me to actually begin the process of writing this book, my wistful dream for several years. Her gentle guidance throughout the process is immeasurable. With her passion for excellence, she sometimes challenged me to dig a little deeper, to write another paragraph—but always with a beautiful smile tempered with a loving attitude and an eye for perfection.

To SaraBeth Fillingane, cookbook designer extraordinaire, for using her talents to make this cookbook beautiful as well as functional.

To Lori Linenberger, my copyeditor, who spent hours reading the manuscript for clarity and polishing my words while keeping my "voice."

To Wichita Area Sister Cities who arranged a French culinary exchange between Atelier-Cuisine de Laurence in Orléans and *Cooking at Bonnie's Place* in Wichita. As the first part of the exchange, I traveled to France and taught in Laurence Herve's cooking school while being a guest in her home. A few months later, Laurence came to Wichita to visit me and taught a French cooking class at my school. New friendships developed and great memories were made - thanks to the Wichita Areas Sister Cities for this opportunity.

To photographer Gary Krohe, who alongside with RoxAnn, spent endless hours staging and photographing food for the book—thanks for the gorgeous photographs!

To photographer Jeff Tuttle for capturing the essence of my cooking classes on the back cover.

To Bev Swisher and Paula Savage who assisted during the photograph sessions, helping me with the food styling, keeping the kitchen orderly, and for their constant loyal support.

To granddaughters, Stephanie Aeschliman and Hayden Aeschliman, who gave up a few days of their summer vacation to help with testing recipes for the book, assisting during photo shoots and washing loads of dishes.

To my sister Kay Dawson and sister-in-law Barbara Ledbetter who spent many hours doing the preliminary proofing of the initial manuscript and getting the job done quickly and thoroughly.

To friends who spent hours proofreading the manuscript: Kathy Allen, Sherrie Andersen, Hetty Bailey, Melissa Bartel, Kenra Black, Ann Brillhart, Helen Bullock, Donna Depew, Gail Derreberry, RoxAnn Banks Dicker, Dee Dunlap, Connie George, Bobbie Givens, Kenna Gwaltney, Margie Hale, Chris Hamman, Marci Hawks, Judy Hess, Jill Koehn, Pat Leiker, Janie Moore, Ragene Moore, Sue Oswald, Pamela Pancake, Terri Ramseyer, Dyane Razook, Kim Rosen, Sid Row, Susie Steed, Bev Swisher, Laura Tuttle, Sandy Wendt and Vesta York.

To my children and grandchildren who have sampled recipes over and over while I perfected them for the cooking classes. I did not think it was a difficult task until my son Eddie pointed out that once I had the recipe perfected, he never saw it again because I was off testing another one that he had to evaluate. His complaint was he had to consume the tests—never the perfected product.

Since this book is a result of the many cooking classes I have taught, I have been blessed with wonderful assistants who have kept the cooking classes moving smoothly and have made me look better than I really am. Much credit goes to Bev Swisher, Marci Hawks, Rosemary Bartel, Abbie Kerr, Paula Savage, Judith Dobson and Sally O'Donnell who have been loyal friends and pitched in and helped whenever needed.

Gratefully,

Bonnie

Above: When I was a child, Grandpa Ledbetter started me on my collection of this beautiful Floragold depression glass. During the Depression, a coffee cup and saucer were given as a premium for each pound of coffee purchased. Grandpa drank a lot of coffee, and over time, he had stacked up several sets. He gave each of his grand children a set of cups and saucers. Little did we know that one day these dishes would become collectible. Over the years, I have added to the set and my sweet memories of Grandpa Tom are far more valuable than the actual dishes.

Toasted Teriyaki Chicken Quesadillas with Mango Red
   Pepper Salsa 120
Roast Chicken with Herb Butter, Carrots and Onions 127

Chicken Asiago Spedini 86
Chicken Florentine Phyllo Pie 194
Chipotle Glazed Roasted Pork Tenderloin 57

CHOCOLATE
Bonnie's Chocolate Sauce 103
Chocolate Babycakes 207
Chocolate Glazed Irish Cream Cheesecake 214
Chocolate Hazelnut Torte 88
Chocolate Molten Lava Cakes with Vanilla Custard Sauce
and Raspberry Coulis 110
Fresh Churned Strawberry Gelato with Chocolate
   Hazelnut Sauce 22
Hazelnut White Chocolate Cheesecake 164
Lone Star Sheet Cake with Chocolate Pecan Frosting 95
Pot de Crème with White Chocolate Whipped Cream 129
White Chocolate Banana Cream Pie in Almond Crust 136
White Chocolate Raspberry Tiramisu with
   Chocolate Leaves 180

Chocolate Babycakes 207
Chocolate Glazed Irish Cream Cheesecake 214
Chocolate Hazelnut Torte 88
Chocolate Molten Lava Cakes with Vanilla Custard Sauce
and Raspberry Coulis 110
Cilantro Rice 102
Cinnamon and Pecan Roasted Apples 185
Classic Kentucky Hot Browns 186
Coco Lopez Soufflé 123

COCONUT
Cilantro Rice 102
Coco Lopez Soufflé 123
Coconut Cilantro Rice 44
Key Lime Bars 73
Key Lime Tart in Coconut Crust 45

Coconut Cilantro Rice 44

COOKIES
Chocolate Babycakes 207
Key Lime Bars 73
Turtle Bars 151
Ultimate Cranberry Bars 206

CORN
Avocado, Tomato and Corn Salad 98
Black Bean and Corn Salsa 92
Cornbread Wedges with Scallions and Bacon 149
Roasted Corn, Zucchini and Chiles in Lime Butter 122
Roasted Corn, Zucchini, Peppers and Tomatoes 58

Cornbread Wedges with Scallions and Bacon 149

CRAB
Crab Cakes with Baby Greens and Lemon Dill
   Vinaigrette 210
Legendary Crab Rounds 201

Crab Cakes with Baby Greens and Lemon Dill
   Vinaigrette 210

CRANBERRY
Cranberry Apricot Chutney 156
Cranberry Streusel Muffins 193

Mixed Greens with Vinaigrette, Bacon, Sliced Eggs and
   Dried Cranberries 184
Smokin' Chile Pork Tenderloin with Cranberry
   Jezebel Sauce 121
Ultimate Cranberry Bars 206
Wild Rice with Dried Cranberries and Almonds 161

Cranberry Apricot Chutney 156
Cranberry Streusel Muffins 193
Cream of Carrot Soup 27
Cream of Watercress Soup 26
Creamed New Potatoes and Peas 29
Creamy Garlic Spinach 108

CRISPS AND COBBLER
Rustic Blackberry Cobbler 80

Crusty Garlic Cheese Herb Bread 143
Cuban Black Beans with Tomato Salsa 44

DESSERTS
Blackberry Rippled Baked Alaska 38
Coco Lopez Soufflé 123
Fresh Churned Strawberry Gelato with Chocolate
   Hazelnut Sauce 22
Frozen Texas Tumbleweeds 103
Hot Lemon Soufflé with Raspberry Sauce 157
Individual Apple Tarts 117
Peach Melba Tart 66
Pistachio Gelato 53
Pot de Crème with White Chocolate Whipped Cream 129
Pumpkin Caramel Flan 59
Rustic Blackberry Cobbler 80
Vanilla Bean Panna Cotta with Honey Berry Sauce 145
White Chocolate Raspberry Tiramisu with
   Chocolate Leaves 180

Cuban Black Beans with Tomato Salsa 44
Deviled Eggs with Ham 195

DIPS
Shrimp Shooters with Spicy Dipping Sauce 201
Mediterranean Layered Dip 200
Warm Pepper Jack Dip 149
Warm Spinach Dip with Toasted Baguette Slices 203

EGG DISHES
Deviled Eggs with Ham 195
Mixed Greens with Vinaigrette, Bacon, Sliced Eggs and
   Dried Cranberries 184

Farmers' Market Salad with Garlic Goat Cheese
   Medallions 76
Festive Fresh Fruit Salad 192

FISH *(See also Salmon; Shrimp; Trout)*
Crab Cakes with Baby Greens and Lemon Dill
   Vinaigrette 210
Legendary Crab Rounds 201
Roasted Salmon Roulade with Spinach Feta Filling 37
Roasted Salmon with Lemon Butter Sauce 63
Savory Smoked Salmon Torte 205
Shrimp Shooters with Spicy Dipping Sauce 201
Smoked Salmon Cucumber Canapés 49
Tiki Bar Salad with Panko-Crusted Key West Shrimp 41

French Onion Soup 126
Fresh Churned Strawberry Gelato with Chocolate
   Hazelnut Sauce 22
Fresh Fruit in Vanilla Bean Sauce 72

PECAN
Quick Orange Glazed Pecans 49
Spinach Salad with Gorgonzola, Spiced Pecans and
      Warm Sherry Vinaigrette 160

Pesto Garlic Bread 77

PIES
Chicken Florentine Phyllo Pie 194
White Chocolate Banana Cream Pie in Almond Crust 136

Pike County Fried Apples 133
Pistachio Gelato 53
Porcini Mushroom Risotto 19

PORK
Chipotle Glazed Roasted Pork Tenderloin 57
Deviled Eggs with Ham 195
Marinated Thick Pork Chops with Pan Sauce 135
Orange Glazed Baked Ham 28
Roasted Loin of Pork with Blackberry Reduction 163
Roasted Rosemary and Sage Tenderloin of Pork 21
Sherried Mushroom, Ham and Wild Rice Soup 132
Smokin' Chile Pork Tenderloin with Cranberry
      Jezebel Sauce 121
Sweet and Spicy Glazed Pork Tenderloin 43

Pot de Crème with White Chocolate Whipped Cream 129

POTATO
Creamed New Potatoes and Peas 29
Garlic Mashed Potatoes 116
New Potatoes in Dill and Chive Sauce 64
New Potatoes Stuffed with Bacon, Cheese and Chives 204
Potatoes Dauphinois 128
Potatoes Soufflé Gratinée 179
Roasted New Potatoes with Horseradish 79
Roasted Potatoes with Herbs 107
Roasted Loin of Pork with Blackberry Reduction 163
Tall Texas Tater Towers 94

Potatoes Dauphinois 128
Potatoes Soufflé Gratinée 179
Pumpkin Caramel Flan 59

POULTRY (See Chicken; Turkey)

QUESADILLA
Sausage Quesadillas with Black Bean Salsa 99
Toasted Teriyaki Chicken Quesadillas with Mango Red
      Pepper Salsa 120

Quick Orange Glazed Pecans 49

RASPBERRY
Chocolate Molten Lava Cakes with Vanilla Custard Sauce
and Raspberry Coulis 110
Hot Ham Canapés with Raspberry Chipotle Sauce 204
Hot Lemon Soufflé with Raspberry Sauce 157
White Chocolate Raspberry Tiramisu with
      Chocolate Leaves 180

RICE
Cilantro Rice 102
Coconut Cilantro Rice 44
Mexican Rice Risotto 58
Porcini Mushroom Risotto 19
Sherried Mushroom, Ham and Wild Rice Soup 132
Wild Rice and Vegetable Pilaf 155
Wild Rice with Dried Cranberries and Almonds 161

Roast Chicken with Herb Butter, Carrots and Onions 127
Roasted Butternut Squash Soup with Thyme and
      Cider Cream 154
Roasted Corn, Zucchini and Chiles in Lime Butter 122
Roasted Corn, Zucchini, Peppers and Tomatoes 58
Roasted Loin of Pork with Blackberry Reduction 163
Roasted New Potatoes with Horseradish 79
Roasted Potatoes with Herbs 107
Roasted Rosemary and Sage Tenderloin of Pork 21
Roasted Salmon Roulade with Spinach Feta Filling 37
Roasted Salmon with Lemon Butter Sauce 63
Romaine, Tomato and Artichoke Salad 169
Rosemary Focaccia 172
Rosemary Spiced Nuts 202
Ruby Slipper Sippers 184
Rustic Blackberry Cobbler 80

SALAD
Avocado, Tomato and Corn Salad 98
Farmers' Market Salad with Garlic Goat Cheese
      Medallions 76
Festive Fresh Fruit Salad 192
Goat Cheese "Bricks" with Classic Vinaigrette Salad 114
Jicama, Orange and Red Onion Salad with Mango
      Dressing 56
Marinated Artichoke Vegetable Salad 72
Mixed Greens with Vinaigrette, Bacon, Sliced Eggs and
      Dried Cranberries 184
Mixed Greens with Warm Brie Fondue and Winter
      Pear Slices 176
Romaine, Tomato and Artichoke Salad 169
Panzanella Salad 62
Sicilian Garden Salad with Italian Vinaigrette 140
Spinach Salad with Gorgonzola, Spiced Pecans and
      Warm Sherry Vinaigrette 160
Southwest Chopped Salad 148
Tarragon Chicken Salad 50
Texas Slaw 92
Thai-Style Chicken Salad in Wonton Cups 202
Tiki Bar Salad with Panko-Crusted Key West Shrimp
Tossed Green Salad with Orange Vinaigrette 35

SALMON
Mixed Greens with Warm Brie Fondue and Winter
      Pear Slices 176
Roasted Salmon Roulade with Spinach Feta Filling 37
Roasted Salmon with Lemon Butter Sauce 63
Savory Smoked Salmon Torte 205
Smoked Salmon Cucumber Canapés 49

SANDWICHES
Classic Kentucky Hot Browns 186
New Orleans Muffuletta 71
Sausage Quesadillas with Black Bean Salsa 99
Toasted Teriyaki Chicken Quesadillas with Mango Red
      Pepper Salsa 120

SAUCES, DESSERT
Bonnie's Chocolate Sauce 103
Chocolate Molten Lava Cakes with Vanilla Custard Sauce
      and Raspberry Coulis 110
Hot Lemon Soufflé with Raspberry Sauce 157
Vanilla Bean Panna Cotta with Honey Berry Sauce 145

SAUCES, SAVORY
Basil Pesto 77
Black Bean and Corn Salsa 92
Herb Roasted Beef Tenderloin with Mushroom
      Gorgonzola Sauce 178

New Potatoes in Dill and Chive Sauce 64
Northern Italian Chicken Cannelloni with Two Sauces 170
Oven-Roasted Italian Meatballs in Long-Simmered
         Ragu Sauce 142
Roasted Salmon with Lemon Butter Sauce 63
Shredded Beef Enchiladas with Salsa Verde 100
Shrimp Shooters with Spicy Dipping Sauce 201
Smokin' Chile Pork Tenderloin with Cranberry
         Jezebel Sauce 121
Toasted Ravioli with Spicy Red Sauce 140

SAUSAGE
Sausage Quesadillas with Black Bean Salsa 99

Sausage Quesadillas with Black Bean Salsa 99
Sautéed Green Beans with Bacon, Shallots and
         Mushrooms 213
Sautéed Summer Squash with Olives and Parmesan 85
Sautéed Zucchini and Grape Tomatoes 65
Savory Smoked Salmon Torte 205
Sherried Mushroom, Ham and Wild Rice Soup 132
Shredded Beef Enchiladas with Salsa Verde 100

SHRIMP
Shrimp Shooters with Spicy Dipping Sauce 201
Tiki Bar Salad with Panko-Crusted Key West Shrimp 41

Shrimp Shooters with Spicy Dipping Sauce 201
Sicilian Garden Salad with Italian Vinaigrette 140

SIDE DISHES
Avocado, Tomato and Corn Salad 98
Black Bean and Corn Salsa 92
Broccoli with Toasted Garlic Crumbs 133
Cauliflower Broccoli Gratin with Walnuts 162
Cheese Ravioli with Garden-Ripe Tomatoes and
         Spinach 87
Cilantro Rice 102
Cinnamon and Pecan Roasted Apples 185
Coconut Cilantro Rice 44
Cranberry Apricot Chutney 156
Creamed New Potatoes and Peas 29
Creamy Garlic Spinach 108
Cuban Black Beans with Tomato Salsa 44
Fresh Green Beans Almondine 35
Garlic Mashed Potatoes 116
Golden Potato Gratin with Goat Cheese and Herbs 213
Green Bean Carrot Bundles with Bacon 177
Mexican Rice Risotto 58
New Potatoes in Dill and Chive Sauce 64
Orzo Parmesan with Basil, Scallions and Peppers 36
Oven Roasted Vegetables 20
Pike County Fried Apples 133
Porcini Mushroom Risotto 19
Potatoes Dauphinois 128
Potatoes Soufflé Gratinée 179
Roasted Corn, Zucchini and Chiles in Lime Butter 122
Roasted Corn, Zucchini, Peppers and Tomatoes 58
Roasted New Potatoes with Horseradish 79
Roasted Potatoes with Herbs 107
Sautéed Green Beans with Bacon, Shallots and
         Mushrooms 213
Sautéed Summer Squash with Olives and Parmesan 85
Sautéed Zucchini and Grape Tomatoes 65
Steamed Asparagus with Tomato Herb Salsa 30
Tall Texas Tater Towers 94
Texas Slaw 92
Vanilla Roasted Sweet Potato Wedges 122
Wild Rice and Vegetable Pilaf 155
Wild Rice with Dried Cranberries and Almonds 161

Zucchini and Sun-dried Tomato Tart 51

Smoked and Slow-Braised Oven Barbecued
         Beef Brisket 93
Smoked Salmon Cucumber Canapés 49
Smokin' Chile Pork Tenderloin with Cranberry
         Jezebel Sauce 121

SOUPS/STEWS
Bonnie's Quick and Easy Chili 150
Chef Claudio's Barley and Black-Eyed Pea Soup 18
Cream of Carrot Soup 27
Cream of Watercress Soup 26
French Onion Soup 126
Pasta Fagiola 168
Roasted Butternut Squash Soup with Thyme and
         Cider Cream 154
Sherried Mushroom, Ham and Wild Rice Soup 132
Spicy Spanish Gazpacho 70

Southwest Chopped Salad 148
Spicy Spanish Gazpacho 70

SPINACH
Roasted Salmon Roulade with Spinach Feta Filling 37
Spinach Salad with Gorgonzola, Spiced Pecans and Warm
Sherry Vinaigrette 160
Warm Spinach Dip with Toasted Baguette Slices 203

Spinach Salad with Gorgonzola, Spiced Pecans and
         Warm Sherry Vinaigrette 160

SQUASH
Roasted Butternut Squash Soup with Thyme and
         Cider Cream 154
Roasted Corn, Zucchini and Chiles in Lime Butter 122
Roasted Corn, Zucchini, Peppers and Tomatoes 58
Sautéed Summer Squash with Olives and Parmesan 85
Sautéed Zucchini and Grape Tomatoes 65
Zucchini and Sun-dried Tomato Tart 51

Steamed Asparagus with Tomato Herb Salsa 30
Strawberries and Cream Cake 31

STRAWBERRY
Fresh Churned Strawberry Gelato with Chocolate
         Hazelnut Sauce 22
Strawberries and Cream Cake 31

SWEET POTATO
Vanilla Roasted Sweet Potato Wedges 122

Tall Texas Tater Towers 94
Tarragon Chicken Salad 50
Texas Slaw 92
Thai-Style Chicken Salad in Wonton Cups 202
Tiki Bar Salad with Panko-Crusted Key West Shrimp 41
Toasted Ravioli with Spicy Red Sauce 140
Toasted Teriyaki Chicken Quesadillas with Mango Red
         Pepper Salsa 120

TOMATO
Avocado, Tomato and Corn Salad 98
Panzanella Salad 62
Roasted Corn, Zucchini, Peppers and Tomatoes 58
Romaine, Tomato and Artichoke Salad 169
Sautéed Zucchini and Grape Tomatoes 65
Steamed Asparagus with Tomato Herb Salsa 30
Zucchini and Sun-dried Tomato Tart 51

VEGETABLES

THANK YOU for joining me on this culinary journey. I hope it has been a joy for you.

For information regarding my cooking classes and to view the latest schedule for *Cooking at Bonnie's Place*, please go to www.cookingatbonnies.com

If you would like to order additional copies of this book, you may order from www.farmtofrance.com, or contact me at:

BONNIE AESCHLIMAN
COOKING AT BONNIE'S PLACE
9747 EAST 21st STREET, SUITE 139
WICHITA, KANSAS 67206
316.425.5224

HAPPY COOKING!

Bonnie